Woodworking Projects: Furniture & Accessories

Complete Handyman's Library™
Handyman Club of America
Minneapolis, Minnesota

Published in 1997 by
Handyman Club of America
12301 Whitewater Drive
Minnetonka, Minnesota 55343

Published by arrangement with Cowles Creative Publishing, Inc.
ISBN 0-86573-657-x

Printed on American paper by
R. R. Donnelley & Sons Co.
99 98 97 / 5 4 3 2 1

CREDITS:
Created by: The Editors of Cowles Creative Publishing
and the staff of the Handyman Club of America
in cooperation with Black & Decker. **BLACK&DECKER**
is a trademark of Black & Decker (US), Incorporated
and is used under license.

Handyman Club of America:
*Vice President, Products & Business
Development:* Mike Vail
Book Products Development Manager: Mark Johanson
Book Marketing Coordinator: Jay McNaughton

Contents

Introduction

Making woodworking projects is a delightful activity, particularly when the results are attractive and functional. And you often can create these objects at a fraction of the price for similar but inferior pieces found in stores.

Woodworking Projects: Furniture & Accessories is full of useful projects to enhance the appeal and efficiency of your home. A variety of durable, attractive storage ideas are presented, so you can display collectibles, books or kitchen plates, utensils, and pots and pans proudly, yet keep them safely out of the way. Or build decorative projects that increase the beauty and function of your living spaces. Additional projects include a footstool for hard-to-reach areas and a utility cart for making your yard and garden projects easier to accomplish. Larger projects range from a twin bed frame for a kid's room to a handsome oak gateleg dining table.

Every project in *Woodworking Projects: Furniture & Accessories* can be built using only basic hand tools and portable power tools that you probably already own. You don't need a lot of experience, but if you haven't used any of the tools before, it's best to first practice using them on scraps of wood. And you won't spend hours scouring specialty stores for necessary materials. We used only common products sold in most building centers and corner hardware stores to make these items.

For each of the projects in this book, you will find a complete cutting list, a lumber-shopping list, a detailed construction drawing, full-color photographs of major steps, and clear, easy-to-follow directions that guide you through every step of the project.

Organizing Your Worksite

Portable power tools and hand tools offer a level of convenience that is a great advantage over stationary power tools. But using them safely and conveniently requires some basic housekeeping. Whether you are working in a garage, a basement or outdoors, it is important that you establish a flat, dry holding area where you can store tools. Set aside a piece of plywood on sawhorses, or dedicate an area of your workbench for tool storage, and be sure to return tools to that area once you are finished with them. It is also important that all waste, including lumber scraps and sawdust, be disposed of in a timely fashion. Check with your local waste disposal department before throwing away any large scraps of building materials or any finishing-material containers.

Safety Tips
•*Always wear eye and hearing protection when operating power tools and performing any other dangerous activities.*
•*Choose a well-ventilated work area when cutting or shaping wood and when using finishing products.*

Tools & Materials

At the start of each project, you will find a set of symbols that show which power tools are used to complete the project as it is shown (see below). You will also need a set of basic hand tools: a hammer, screwdrivers, tape measure, a level, a combination square, C-clamps, and pipe or bar clamps. You will also find a shopping list of all the construction materials you will need. Miscellaneous materials and hardware are listed with the cutting list that accompanies the construction drawing. When buying lumber, note that the "nominal" size of the lumber is usually larger than the "actual size." For example, a 2 × 4 is actually $1\frac{1}{2} \times 3\frac{1}{2}$".

Power Tools You Will Use

Circular saw *to make straight cuts. For long cuts and rip-cuts, use a straight-edge guide. Install a carbide-tipped combination blade for most projects.*

Drills: *use a cordless drill for drilling pilot holes and counterbores, and to drive screws; use an electric drill for sanding and grinding tasks.*

Jig saw *for making contoured cuts and internal cuts. Use a combination wood blade for most projects where you will cut pine, cedar or plywood.*

Power sander *to prepare wood for a finish and to smooth out sharp edges. Owning several power sanders ($\frac{1}{3}$-sheet, $\frac{1}{4}$-sheet, and belt) is helpful.*

Belt sander *for resurfacing rough wood. Can also be used as a stationary sander when mounted on its side on a flat worksurface.*

Router *to cut decorative edges and roundovers in wood. As you gain more experience, use routers for cutting grooves (like dadoes) to form joints.*

Guide to Building Materials Used in This Book

•Sheet goods:
OAK PLYWOOD: *Oak-veneered plywood commonly sold in ¾" and ¼" thicknesses. Fairly expensive.*
BIRCH PLYWOOD: *A workable, readily available alternative to pine or fir plywood. Has smooth surface excellent for painting or staining; few voids in the edges. Moderately expensive.*
MELAMINE BOARD: *Particleboard with a glossy, polymerized surface that is water-resistant and easy to clean. Inexpensive.*
MDF (MEDIUM-DENSITY FIBERBOARD): *Plywood with a pressed-wood core that is well suited for shaping. Moderately inexpensive.*
PINE PANELS: *Pine boards glued together, cut and sanded. Varying thicknesses, usually ⅝" or ¾".*
HARDBOARD: *Dense particleboard with a smooth surface used for backing. Very inexpensive.*

•Dimension lumber:
PINE: *A basic, versatile softwood. "Select" and "#2 or better" are suitable grades. Relatively inexpensive.*
RED OAK: *A common hardwood that stains well and is very durable. Relatively inexpensive.*
BIRCH: *A common hardwood without much visible grain that paints well. Relatively inexpensive.*
CEDAR: *Naturally moisture-resistant. Moderately expensive.*

Guide to Fasteners & Adhesives Used in This Book

•Fasteners & hardware:
WOOD SCREWS: *Brass or steel; most projects use screws with a #6 or #8 shank. Can be driven with a power driver.*
NAILS & BRADS: *Finish nails can be set below the wood surface: common (box) nails have wide, flat heads; brads or wire nails are very small, thin fasteners with small heads.*
MISCELLANEOUS HARDWARE: *Drawer pulls; outdoor light fixture; magnetic door catches; plastic or rubber feet.*

•Adhesives:
MOISTURE-RESISTANT WOOD GLUE: *Any exterior wood glue, such as plastic resin glue.*
TILE ADHESIVE: *An adhesive specially designed for ceramic tile.*

•Miscellaneous materials:
Wood plugs; dowels; ceramic tile; acrylic; Plexiglas®; trim moldings; veneer tape; fiberglass screen fabric; others as required.

Finishing Your Project

Before applying finishing materials, fill nail holes and blemishes with wood putty or filler. Also, fill all voids in the edges of any exposed plywood with wood putty. Insert wood plugs into counterbore holes, then sand until the plug is level with the wood. Sand wood surfaces with medium sandpaper (100- or 120-grit), then finish-sand with fine sandpaper (150- or 180-grit). Wipe off residue, and apply the finish of your choice. Apply two or three thin coats of a hard, protective topcoat, like polyurethane, over painted or stained wood.

Dry Sink

This classic cabinet brings antique charm to any setting.

CONSTRUCTION MATERIALS

Quantity	Lumber
4	1 × 2" × 6' birch
5	1 × 3" × 8' birch
1	1 × 4" × 8' birch
2	1 × 6" × 6' birch
1	½" × 4 × 4' birch plywood
1	¾" × 4 × 8' birch plywood
3	⅜" × 4' birch dowling

A traditional dry sink was used to hold a wash-basin in the days before indoor plumbing, but today it can serve a variety of decorative and practical functions around the house. Our classic dry sink is used as a garden potting table. It's the ideal height for mixing soils, planting seeds and watering plants. The top has a handy back shelf to hold plants and accessories, while the curved front and sides are especially designed to contain messy spills. The roomy cabinet has two hinged doors for easy access and enough interior space to store pots, planters, fertilizers, insecticides and an assortment of gardening tools. This project features birch plywood panels with solid birch frames secured with strong "through-dowel" joinery.

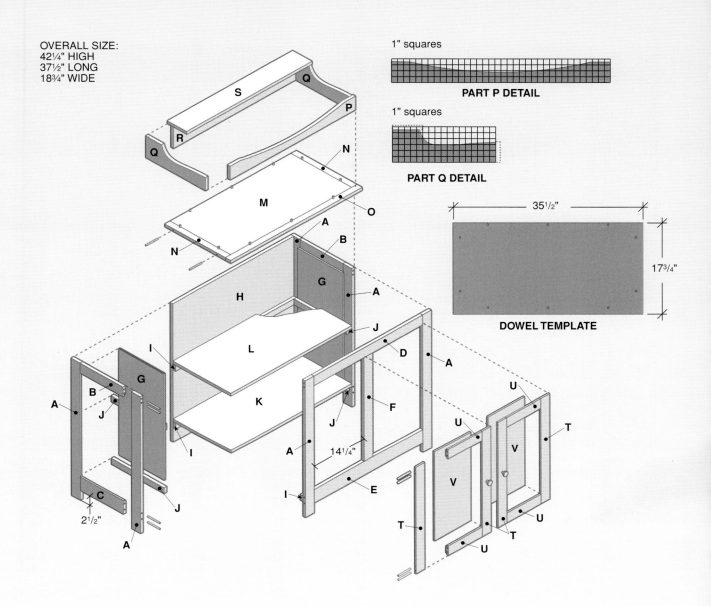

OVERALL SIZE:
42¼" HIGH
37½" LONG
18¾" WIDE

1" squares

PART P DETAIL

1" squares

PART Q DETAIL

35½"

17¾"

DOWEL TEMPLATE

2½"

14¼"

Cutting List					Cutting List			
Key	**Part**	**Dimension**	**Pcs.**	**Material**	**Key**	**Part**	**Dimension**	**Pcs.**	**Material**
A	Stile	¾ × 2½ × 35¼"	6	Birch	**L**	Shelf	¾ × 16⅜ × 34⅜"	1	Birch ply.
B	Side rail, top	¾ × 2½ × 12¼"	2	Birch	**M**	Top	¾ × 17¼ × 34½"	1	Birch ply.
C	Side rail, bottom	¾ × 3½ × 12¼"	2	Birch	**N**	Top side edge	¾ × 1½ × 17¼"	2	Birch
D	Front rail, top	¾ × 2½ × 31"	1	Birch	**O**	Top front edge	¾ × 1½ × 37½"	1	Birch
E	Front rail, bottom	¾ × 3½ × 31"	1	Birch	**P**	Top assem. front	¾ × 3½ × 35¾"	1	Birch
F	Mullion	¾ × 2½ × 26¾"	1	Birch	**Q**	Top assem. side	¾ × 5½ × 17"	2	Birch
G	Side panel	½ × 12⅝ × 27½"	2	Birch ply.	**R**	Top assem. back	¾ × 5½ × 34"	1	Birch
H	Back panel	¾ × 34½ × 35¼"	1	Birch ply.	**S**	Top assem. cap	¾ × 5½ × 35¾"	1	Birch
I	Back, front cleat	¾ × 1½ × 34½"	3	Birch	**T**	Door stile	¾ × 2½ × 27¼"	4	Birch
J	Side cleat	¾ × 1½ × 15"	4	Birch	**U**	Door rail	¾ × 2½ × 9¾"	4	Birch
K	Bottom	¾ × 16½ × 34⅜"	1	Birch ply.	**V**	Door panel	½ × 10½ × 23"	2	Birch ply.

Materials: Wood glue, birch shelf nosing (⅛ × ⅜ × 34½"), 16-ga. brads, #8 wood screws (1¼", 1⅝"), 4d finish nails, ⅜ × 1" dowels (10), door pulls (2), finishing materials.

Note: Measurements reflect the actual thickness of dimensional lumber.

7

A

Drill holes and insert the dowels after the frame pieces have been glued together.

B

Carefully square the corners of the rabbets in the side panels and door panels, using a sharp chisel.

Directions: Dry Sink

CUT AND ASSEMBLE THE CABINET FRAMES. The dry sink is built with two side frames, a face frame and two door frames—all made from birch rails and stiles joined with "through" dowels.

Begin by cutting the stiles (A) and rails (B, C, D, E) and mullion (F) to length.

Build each side frame by gluing a top and bottom side rail between two stiles. The bottom rail should be raised 2½" from the bottoms of the stiles. Clamp in place, check for square and let dry.

After the glue has dried, drill two ⅜"-dia. × 3"-deep holes through the stiles at each rail location **(photo A).** Cut 3"-long dowels, and score a groove along one side. Apply glue to the dowels, then use a mallet to drive them into the holes.

Repeat this process to construct the front frame, using two stiles, the top and bottom front rails, and the mullion. Make sure the mullion is centered between the stiles.

Cut the door frame stiles (T) and rails (U) to size with a circular saw, and assemble frame parts in a similar fashion.

Drill pilot holes, and attach cleats with wood screws to the frame but not into the ½" panel.

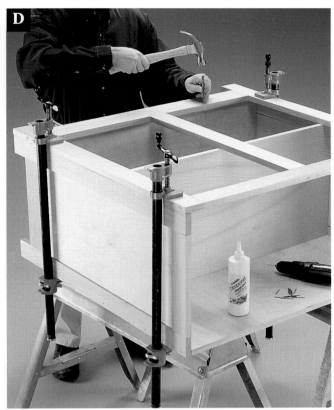

Clamp one side of the face frame and check for square, then clamp the other side and check for square again. Attach with finish nails and set.

ADD THE PANELS. The ½" plywood side panels and door panels fit into rabbets cut around the inside of the side frames and door frames.

Mount a ⅜" rabbet bit in your router, set to ½" depth. Cut a continuous rabbet around the inside of the side frames. Square off the corners of the rabbet, using a chisel **(photo B).** On the back face of each door frame, cut a rabbet around the inside of the frame in a similar fashion.

Next, change the depth of the router bit to ⅜", and cut another rabbet around the outside edge of the door frame. This creates a lip which will overlap the face frame when the doors are attached.

Cut the side panels (G) and the door panels (V) to size. Position each panel inside its frame, then drill pilot holes and attach the panels with 16-ga. brads. Position and attach hinges and knobs on the cabinet doors.

PREPARE THE REMAINING PIECES. Cut the back panel (H), bottom (K) and shelf (L) to size. Cut and attach shelf nosing to the front edge of the shelf, using glue and brads.

Cut the front and back cleats (I) and side cleats (J) to size. On the inside faces of the face frame stiles, mark reference lines 5¼" from the bottom. On the inside faces of the back panel and side frame stiles, mark reference lines at 5¼" and 21" from the bottom.

To attach the side cleats, position the cleats with the top edges flush with the reference lines, with the ends of cleats set back ¾" from the front edge and 1½" from the back edge. Drill countersunk pilot holes, and attach the cleats with 1¼" wood screws **(photo C).**
NOTE: Take care to screw the side cleats into the frame members only, not into the ½" panels.

Attach the back cleats to the back panel, and the front cleat to the inside of the face frame,

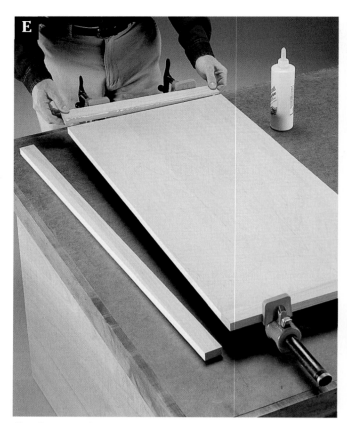

Cut the top side edges and top front edge, and attach the pieces with wood glue. Clamp in place until the glue dries, then drill and insert dowels to strengthen the joints.

When creating the top assembly, first attach the front piece to the sides, then attach the sides to the back, using wood glue and 4d finish nails.

using the same process.

ASSEMBLE THE CABINET. Position the back panel between the side assemblies. Drill countersunk pilot holes, and attach the sides to the back panel with 1⅝" wood screws. Next, position the bottom over the cleats. Check to make sure the cabinet is square, then drill pilot holes and attach the bottom by driving 4d finish nails into the cleats. Position and attach the shelf in the same manner.

Lay the cabinet on its back and clamp the face frame in position. Check for square, then drill pilot holes and attach the face frame to the cabinet with glue and 4d finish nails driven into the side frames,

bottom and shelf **(photo D).** Also drive finish nails through the bottom and into the front cleat. Set all nail heads.

Position and mount the doors in their openings, then remove them and detach the hinges and knobs until the wood has been finished.

ASSEMBLE AND ATTACH THE TOP. Cut cabinet top (M), side edges (N) and front edge (O) to size. Attach the edges around the top, using glue. Clamp the pieces in place until the glue dries **(photo E).** After the glue has dried, drill holes and reinforce the joints with 3"-long dowels, following the same procedure used to construct the cabinet frames.

Position the top on the cabinet, leaving a ¾" overhang on both ends and the front. Drill countersunk pilot holes, and attach the top with glue and 1⅝" wood screws driven into the cabinet frames and back panel.

CREATE THE TOP ASSEMBLY. Cut the top assembly parts (P, Q, R and S) to size. Transfer the patterns to the pieces (see *Diagram*), then cut them out with a jig saw. Sand the cut edges smooth.

Position the front piece against the side pieces, so there is a ⅛" overhang on both ends. Drill pilot holes and attach the front piece to the side pieces with glue and 4d finish nails.

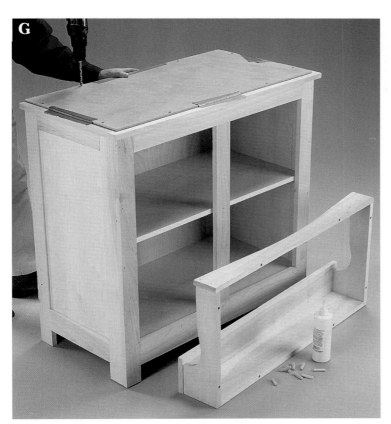

G

Use a template to ensure that the dowel holes in the top assembly will match those drilled in the top of the cabinet.

First, finish-sand all surfaces and edges of the cabinet. Next, stain the entire project (we used medium cherry stain). After the stain dries, apply latex paint to the desired surfaces (we used Glidden® Centurian blue paint, applying it to all surfaces except the top).

While the paint is still damp, use a cloth and denatured alcohol to remove color until you achieve the desired look. To mimic the look of a genuine antique, try to remove most of the paint from the corners and edges, where a cabinet typically receives the most wear. Reinstall the hardware and hang the doors after the finish has dried.

Position the back piece between the sides, then drill pilot holes and attach the pieces with glue and 4d finish nails **(photo F).** Position the cap piece so it overlaps by ⅛" on each end, then drill pilot holes, and attach with glue and 4d finish nails.

ATTACH THE TOP ASSEMBLY. The top assembly is attached to the cabinet with dowels, positioned with the benefit of an easy-to-build template.

Create the template by tracing the outer outline of the top assembly on a piece of scrap plywood or hardboard. Cut the template to this size. Place the template over the bottom of the top assembly, then drill ⅜"-dia. × ½"-deep dowel holes through the template and into the top assembly.

Place the template on the cabinet top, centered side to side with the back edges flush, and tape it in place. Drill corresponding dowel holes into the top **(photo G).** Remove the template and attach the top assembly to the cabinet with glue and 1" dowels. Use weights or clamps to hold the top assembly in place until the glue dries.

FINISH THE CABINET. To give our dry sink a vintage look, we used a unique antiquing method that uses both stain and paint.

Window Seat

*Curl up with a good book,
or just enjoy the view from this cozy window seat.*

CONSTRUCTION MATERIALS

Quantity	Lumber
3	1 × 2" × 8' oak
1	1 × 2" × 6' oak
1	1 × 3" × 6' oak
4	1 × 4" × 6' oak
9	½ × 1¾" × 4' oak*
1	½ × 2¾" × 2' oak*
8	½ × 2¾" × 3' oak*
2	½ × 2¾" × 4' oak*
1	½ × 2¾" × 5' oak*
6	½ × 3¾" × 5' oak*
1	¾" × 2 × 6' oak plywood

*Stock sizes commonly available at most wood-working specialty stores.

You'll find this Mission-style window seat to be an excellent place to spend an afternoon. Though it fits nicely under a window, the frame is wide enough so you won't ever feel cramped. The length is perfect for taking a nap, enjoying a sunset or watching children playing in the yard. Or perhaps you'd prefer to sit elsewhere to simply admire your craftsmanship from a distance.

Our project uses oak for its strength and warm texture, and includes a frame face and nosing trim for a more elegant appearance. The rails are capped to make comfortable armrests, and the back is set lower than the sides so it won't block your window view. Though this project has many parts, it requires few tools and is remarkably easy to build. A few hours of labor will reward you with a delightful place to enjoy many hours of relaxation.

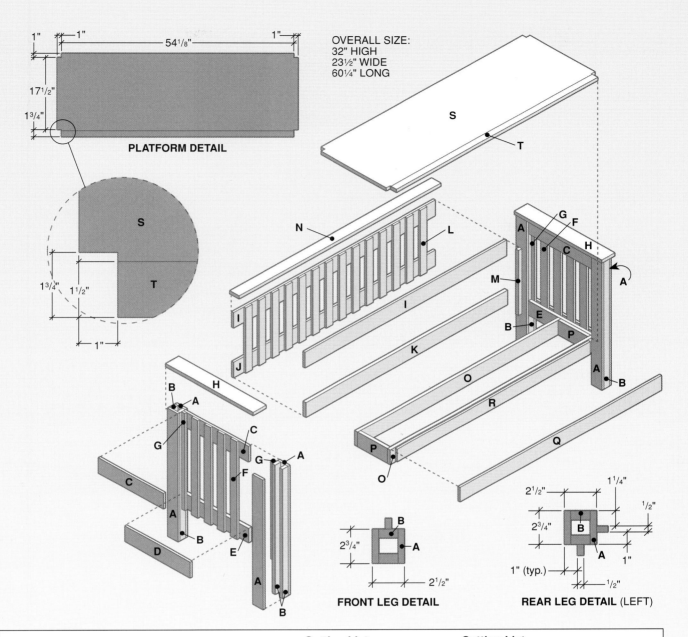

PLATFORM DETAIL

1" 1" 54⅛" 1"

17½"

1¾"

S

T

1¾" 1½"

1"

OVERALL SIZE:
32" HIGH
23½" WIDE
60¼" LONG

S

T

N

L

I

M

G F
A
C H

K

B
E
P
A
B

O
R

Q

H
B
A

G

C

C
G
A

F

A
B

D
E

A

B

FRONT LEG DETAIL

B
A
2¾"
2½"

REAR LEG DETAIL (LEFT)

2½" 1¼"
2¾" ½"
B
A
1" (typ.) 1"
½"

Cutting List				
Key	Part	Dimension	Pcs.	Material
A	Wide leg piece	½ × 2¾ × 31¼"	8	Oak
B	Narrow leg piece	¾ × 1½ × 31¼"	8	Oak
C	End top rail	½ × 3¾ × 17½"	4	Oak
D	Outer bottom rail	½ × 3¾ × 17½"	2	Oak
E	Inner bottom rail	¾ × 3½ × 17½"	2	Oak
F	End slat	½ × 1¾ × 23¾"	8	Oak
G	End half slat	½ × ⅞ × 23¾"	4	Oak
H	End cap	¾ × 3½ × 23½"	2	Oak
I	Back top rail	½ × 3¾ × 54¼"	2	Oak
J	Outer bottom rail	½ × 3¾ × 54¼"	1	Oak

Cutting List				
Key	Part	Dimension	Pcs.	Material
K	Inner bottom rail	¾ × 3½ × 54¼"	1	Oak
L	Back slat	½ × 1¾ × 15¾"	14	Oak
M	Back half slat	½ × ⅞ × 15¾"	2	Oak
N	Back cap	¾ × 2½ × 54¼"	1	Oak
O	Support side	¾ × 3½ × 54¾"	2	Oak
P	Support end	¾ × 3½ × 8"	2	Oak
Q	Frame face	½ × 3¾ × 54¼"	1	Oak
R	Spacer	½ × 2¾ × 52"	1	Oak
S	Platform	¾ × 18¾ × 56⅛"	1	Oak Ply.
T	Platform nosing	¾ × 1½ × 54⅛"	1	Oak

Materials: Wood glue, 1" brads, wood screws (⅝",1¼", 1½"), 4d finish nails, oak-veneer edge tape (8'), finishing materials.
Note: Measurements reflect the actual thickness of dimensional lumber.

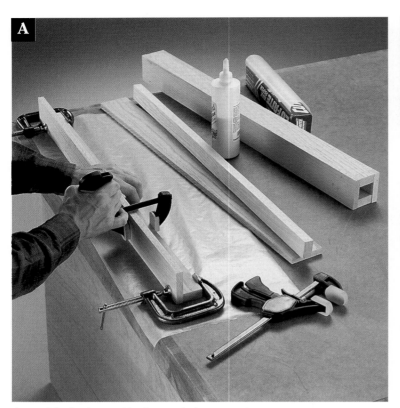

Assemble the legs with glue and clamps, using wax paper to protect your worksurface.

Attach the end slats to the outer rails with glue and wood screws, using a spacer as a guide.

Directions: Window Seat

ASSEMBLE THE LEGS. Each leg piece consists of four pieces glued together.

Cut the wide leg pieces (A) and narrow leg pieces (B) to size, and sand the cut edges smooth. For each leg, lay a narrow leg piece on your worksurface, then butt a wide leg piece against an edge to form an "L." Apply wood glue and clamp the pieces together **(photo A).** Assemble and glue together another "L" in the same fashion. Then, glue the two L-assemblies together to form a leg. Repeat this process to make the other legs.

BUILD THE END ASSEMBLIES. To ensure that the end rails and slats remain square during the assembly process, build a simple jig by attaching two 2 × 2" boards at a 90° angle along adjacent edges of a 24 × 48" piece of plywood.

Begin by cutting the end top rails (C), outer bottom rails (D), inner bottom rails (E) and end slats (F) to size, and sand the edges smooth.

Place a top rail and an outer bottom rail in the jig. Position a slat over the rails, 2⅜" in from the ends. Adjust the pieces so ends of the slat are flush with the edges of the rails, and keep the entire assembly tight against the jig. Attach with glue and ⅝" wood screws driven through countersunk pilot holes.

Using a 1¾"-wide spacer, attach the remaining end slats with glue and ⅝" screws **(photo B).** NOTE: Make sure to test-fit all the slats for uniform spacing before attaching them to the rails.

Now, position a bottom rail over the slats, ¼" up from the bottom edges of the slats, and attach with glue and countersunk 1¼" screws. Place a top rail over the slats and attach with glue and 1" brads.

TIP

Take care to countersink all screw heads completely when building furniture that will be used as seating.

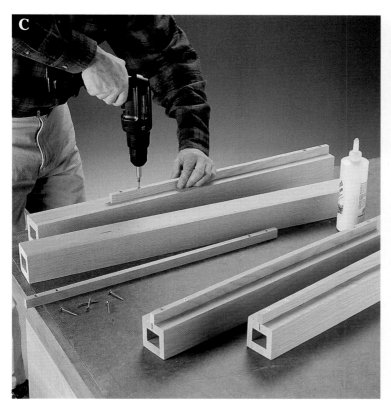

Attach the end half slats to the legs with glue and countersunk wood screws.

Attach the lower inner rail with glue and countersunk screws; the upper inner rail with glue and finish nails.

Repeat the process to build the other end assembly.

BUILD THE BACK ASSEMBLY. The back is constructed in a similar manner to that used for the end assemblies. Again, use the jig to keep the back assembly square.

Cut the back top rails (I), the outer bottom rail (J), the inner bottom rail (K) and the back slats (L) to length and sand the cuts smooth. Place a top rail and the inner bottom rail in the jig. Place a back slat on the rails, 2⅝" in from the ends. Adjust the pieces so the ends of the slat are flush with the edge of the top rail and overhang the edge of the bottom rail by ¼". Attach the slat with glue and ⅝" wood screws driven through countersunk pilot holes.

Test-fit the remaining slats, using a spacer as a guide, then attach with glue and ⅝" wood screws. Position the remaining bottom rail so the edge is flush with the bottom edges of the slats, and attach with glue and 1" brads. Place the remaining top rail over the slats and attach it with glue and 1" brads.

JOIN THE LEGS TO THE END ASSEMBLIES. Half slats attached to the legs will complete the slat pattern and serve as cleats for attaching the end assemblies.

Cut the end half slats (G) to size from ½ × 2¾" × 4' stock and sand smooth. Place each leg on your worksurface with a narrow leg piece facing up. Center the half slat on the face of the leg (see *Diagram*), with the top ends flush. Drill countersunk pilot holes in the half slat, locating them so the screw heads will be covered by the rails when the seat is com

pleted, then attach the half slats to the legs with glue and 1¼" screws **(photo C).**

Position an end assembly between a front and rear leg so the half slats fit between the rails and the top edges are flush. Drill counterbored pilot holes through the inner bottom rail and into the half slats, taking care to avoid other screws, then attach with glue and 1¼" screws. Attach the top rail to the half slats with glue and 4d finish nails driven through pilot holes **(photo D).** Repeat this process for the other end assembly.

MAKE THE SUPPORT FRAME. The support frame is attached to the inner bottom rails on the end assemblies, and will support the seat.

Cut the support sides (O) and ends (P) to length, and

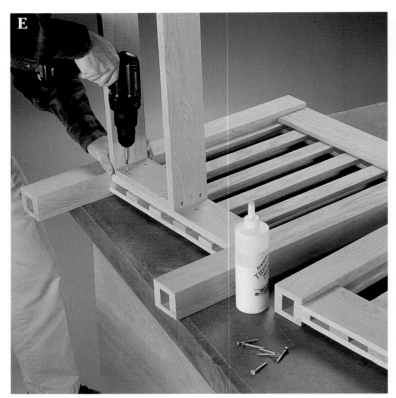

Attach the support frame with glue and countersunk screws driven through the support end and into the inner bottom rail.

Glue the platform nosing to the platform and hold it in place with bar clamps.

sand the cuts smooth. Position the ends between the sides (see *Diagram),* then drill countersunk pilot holes and join the pieces with glue and 1¼" screws.

Lay one end assembly on your worksurface, and position the support frame upright so the front corner of the frame is tight against the front leg and the edges of the frame are flush with the edges of the bottom rail. Drill counterbored pilot holes and attach the support frame to the end assembly with glue and 1¼" screws **(photo E).** Stand the window seat upright, and clamp the other end in position. Drill counterbored pilot holes and attach with 1¼" screws.

ATTACH THE BACK. Like the end assemblies, the back assembly is joined to the legs with half slats.

Cut the back half slats (M) to size from ½ × 2¾" × 2' stock and sand smooth. On the inside face of each rear leg, measure 7½" up from the bottom, and draw a horizontal line at this point. Measure in 1¼" from the back edge of the leg along this line, and draw a vertical line upward.

Position a half slat against the leg so its rear edge is on the vertical line and its bottom edge is on the horizontal line. Drill countersunk pilot holes and attach the half slat to the leg with glue and 1½" screws. Repeat with the other rear leg.

After the half slats have been attached to each rear leg, slide the back assembly over the half slats so the top edges are flush. Drill countersunk pilot holes through the inner bottom rail into the half slat and attach with glue and 1¼" screws. Drill

pilot holes and join the top rail to the back half slats with glue and 4d finish nails.

ATTACH THE CAPS. Caps are attached to the ends and back of the window seat to create armrests and backrests.

Cut the end caps (H) and back cap (N) to length. Center the end caps over the end assemblies, with the back edges flush. Drill counterbored pilot holes through the end caps and into the legs, and attach with glue and 1½" screws.

Position the back cap over the back assembly so the front edge is flush with the front edges of the legs. Drill counterbored pilot holes through the back cap into the top rails. Attach with glue and 1½" screws.

MAKE THE PLATFORM. Because the platform is made of plywood, the edges must be covered with oak nosing and

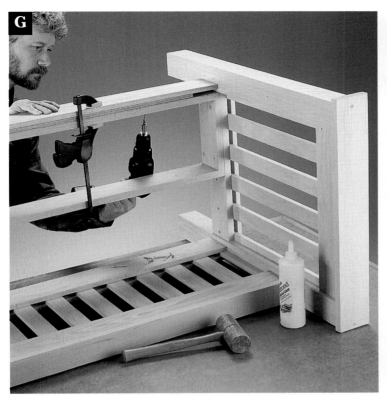

G

H

Clamp the spacer and frame face to the support frame and attach with glue and screws driven through the inside of the support frame.

Attach the platform to the rails, frame face and support frame with glue and counterbored screws.

edge tape to create the appearance of solid wood.

Cut the platform (S) and platform nosing (T) to size, and sand smooth. Glue the nosing to the front edge of the platform, leaving 1" exposed on each end, and clamp in place until the glue dries **(photo F).**

To accommodate the legs, use a jig saw to cut a 1 × 1" notch in each back corner of the platform and a 1 × 1¾" notch in each front corner (see *Diagram).* Apply self-adhesive oak veneer edge tape to the side and back edges of the platform (don't apply tape to the notches). Lightly sand the edges of the tape until they are smooth.

ATTACH THE FRAME FACE. The frame face and spacer are attached to support the front edge of the platform and create design consistency.

First, cut the frame face (Q) and spacer (R) to length, and sand the cuts smooth. Use glue to join the pieces together, centering the spacer on the frame face. Clamp the pieces together until the glue dries.

Position the frame face assembly against the front of the support frame so the top edges of the face and support frame are flush. Drill countersunk pilot holes from inside the support frame, then attach with glue and 1¼" screws **(photo G).**

ATTACH THE PLATFORM. Drill counterbored pilot holes and attach the platform to the support the frame, frame face and bottom rails with glue and 1½" screws **(photo H).**

APPLY FINISHING TOUCHES. Plug the counterbored holes with glued oak plugs and fill all visible nail holes with putty. Scrape off any excess glue and

finish-sand the window seat. Apply a stain of your choice (ours is medium oak), then add a coat of polyurethane.

Add seat cushions that complement the wood tones of the window seat and the overall decorating scheme of your room.

TIP

If you find any nail holes that were not filled before you applied stain and finish, you can go back and fill the holes with a putty stick that closely matches the color of the wood stain.

17

Game Table

Kids will appreciate the size of this table, but the adults will remember the craftsmanship.

CONSTRUCTION MATERIALS

Quantity	Lumber
3	1 × 2" × 8' oak
3	1 × 3" × 8' oak
1	¾" × 2 × 2' MDF*
1	¼" × 2 × 4' hardboard

* Medium-density fiberboard

Our game table is a striking piece of furniture that can easily double as a decorative end table. Sturdy leg units and an internal cleat structure make this table durable and stable enough for constant use. A slim drawer slides underneath the game table, great for holding score pads, cards or other gaming supplies.

The most striking feature of our game table is the veneered top. The pattern is accomplished with four panels of self-adhesive oak veneer applied in different directions for a unique appearance. Rabbet joints cut with a router join the oak border trim to the tabletop.

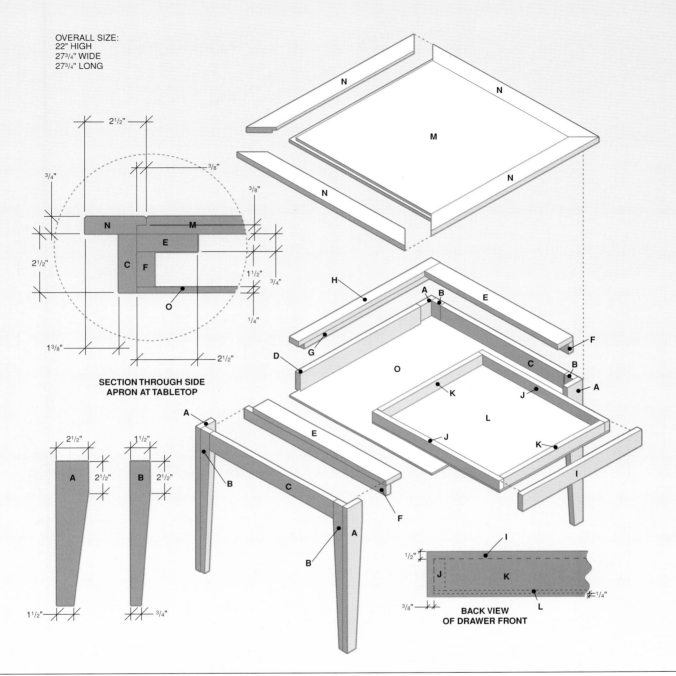

OVERALL SIZE:
22" HIGH
27¾" WIDE
27¾" LONG

SECTION THROUGH SIDE
APRON AT TABLETOP

BACK VIEW
OF DRAWER FRONT

Cutting List

Key	Part	Dimension	Pcs.	Material
A	Wide leg piece	¾ × 2½ × 21¼"	4	Oak
B	Narrow leg piece	¾ × 1½ × 21¼"	4	Oak
C	Side apron	¾ × 2½ × 20½"	2	Oak
D	Back apron	¾ × 2½ × 20"	1	Oak
E	Side stretcher	¾ × 2½ × 22"	2	Oak
F	Side cleat	¾ × 1½ × 23½"	2	Oak
G	Back cleat	¾ × 1½ × 22"	1	Oak
H	Back stretcher	¾ × 1½ × 23½"	1	Oak

Cutting List

Key	Part	Dimension	Pcs.	Material
I	Drawer front	¾ × 2½ × 19¾"	1	Oak
J	Drawer side	¾ × 1½ × 21"	2	Oak
K	Drawer end	¾ × 1½ × 16¾"	2	Oak
L	Drawer bottom	¼ × 18¼ × 21"	1	Hardboard
M	Top	¾ × 23½ × 23½"	1	MDF
N	Trim	¾ × 2½ × 27¾"	4	Oak
O	Bottom	¼ × 23½ × 23½"	1	Hardboard

Materials: Wood glue, #6 × 1¼" wood screws, 4d finish nails, 2 x 3' self-adhesive oak veneer (2), finishing materials.

Note: Measurements reflect the actual thickness of dimensional lumber.

Use a sharp blade to cut the veneer pieces along the template. Press firmly to prevent the veneer from sliding.

Clamp the top securely to your worksurface to keep it from slipping when rabbeting the top.

Directions: Game Table

CUT AND ASSEMBLE THE VENEER. The veneer top of the table consists of four triangular quadrants, requiring two large pieces of veneer. Two quadrants are cut from each piece.

Begin by making an 18 × 18" square template from ¼" scrap hardboard. From one corner of the template, measure 17" along adjoining sides and mark points. Tape the bottom edges of the template to your cutting surface. Slide the sheet of veneer under the template until the sides meet the marks and the veneer is positioned at a 45° angle to the edges of the hardboard. Cut with a utility knife down to the marks **(photo A),** then remove the template and cut between the marks to complete the triangle. Repeat the process to cut the three remaining veneer pieces, always keeping the grain aligned as in photo A. Tape the triangular veneer pieces together on their finished faces so the top points meet.

MAKE THE TOP. Cut the top (M) from MDF. Make sure it is perfectly square. Draw diagonal reference lines connecting opposite corners.

Place the veneer on the top, aligning the veneer seams with the diagonal reference lines. When the veneer is positioned correctly, clamp one side in place, then fold back the opposite half and peel away the backing. Lay the exposed veneer back onto the top, and press to bond. Remove the clamps, fold back the remaining half, peel the backing and apply the veneer. Press all seams firmly in place with a J-roller, and trim the edges.

Rabbet the edge of the top, using your router and a ⅜" self-guiding rabbet bit set to a depth of ⅜" **(photo B).** Also rabbet one edge of the 1 × 3 stock for the trim pieces. Before rabbeting this material, use scrap wood to test-fit the depth of the cut against the rabbeted edges of the top to ensure that the faces will be flush.

Using a block plane or sander, make a ¹⁄₁₆" chamfer (bevel) on the perimeter of the

top and along both upper edges of the 1 × 3. Cut the trim pieces (N) to length, mitering the ends at 45° angles. Attach the trim pieces to the top with glue, and clamp in place. Drill pilot holes and use finish nails to lock-nail the trim pieces together at the joints. Set the nail heads and fill with putty.

MAKE THE LEGS. Cut the wide and narrow leg pieces (A, B) to length. Glue and clamp the edge of each narrow leg piece to the face of a wide piece so the edges are flush **(photo C).** Once dry, mark the diagonal taper on each leg (see *Diagram*), cut with a jig saw and sand smooth.

BUILD THE CLEAT ASSEMBLIES. Cut the side stretchers (E), side cleats (F), back stretcher (H) and back cleat (G) to length. Arrange the side stretchers and cleats in pairs (see *Diagram*). Drill countersunk pilot holes and attach the stretchers to the cleats with glue and screws. Make sure the back cleat is centered on its stretcher, with a ¾" space at each end.

Cleat assembly   Apron

Join the wide and narrow leg pieces with glue; if this is done carefully, no nails or screws are required.

Use glue and screws to join the leg pairs to the cleat assemblies and aprons.

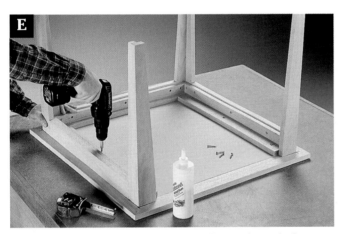

Fasten the top with glue and screws driven through the stretchers and into the top.

ASSEMBLE THE TABLE FRAMEWORK. Cut the side aprons (C) and back apron (D) to length. Lay a side apron on your worksurface, and place the right cleat assembly over it so the side stretcher is standing on edge, flush with the top edge of the apron. Arrange the right front and back legs in their correct position, with the narrow leg pieces flat on the worksurface. The side stretcher should butt against the wide leg pieces, and the side apron should butt against the narrow leg pieces. Make sure the parts are flush on the face and the top edge, then glue and clamp the parts together. Fasten with screws driven through the side cleat into the apron and legs **(photo D).** Repeat the process to assemble the left leg pair.

Position the finished leg pairs upright with the back legs resting on the worksurface. Position the back apron and back cleat assembly between the back legs. Adjust so the edges are flush, and fasten with glue and screws.

ATTACH THE TOP AND BOTTOM. Place the top upside down on a clean worksurface. Set the leg/apron assembly over it, aligning the leg corners on the miter joints. Drill pilot holes and attach the top with glue and screws **(photo E).** Cut the bottom (O) to size, drill pilot holes, and fasten to the bottom edges of the cleats using glue and screws.

BUILD THE DRAWER. Cut all drawer parts (I, J, K, L) to size. Place the drawer ends between the drawer sides so the edges are flush. Drill countersunk pilot holes and attach using glue and screws.

Position the drawer bottom on the drawer box, drill pilot holes, and attach with glue and screws. Lay the drawer front facedown on your worksurface and position the drawer box on it (see *Diagram*). Drill pilot holes, and fasten with glue and screws driven through the end and into the front.

APPLY FINISHING TOUCHES. A water-based finish may loosen the veneer adhesive, so use alkyd-based polyurethane instead. The chamfered joint between the veneer and the top frame may be painted black after the finish has cured.

Jewelry Box

*This piece of fine furniture will
be a worthy home for your family treasures.*

CONSTRUCTION MATERIALS

Quantity	Lumber
1	¾ × 24 × 48" MDF*
1	½ × 12 × 30" birch plywood
1	½ × 24 × 30" birch plywood
1	¼ × 12 × 24" hardboard

*Medium-density fiberboard

Without a suitable home, jewelry has a way of getting lost or misplaced. This elegant and roomy jewelry box solves that problem with pizzazz.

Our classically proportioned chest—like all fine furniture—is as functional as it is beautiful. Three spacious drawers accommodate everything from fun and funky costume jewelry to the finest family heirlooms.

The precision craftsmanship utilizes a simple system of da-does and rabbets to achieve the close tolerances and tight joints which characterize true quality woodwork.

The timeless design of this piece allows for many options in materials and finish, providing great flexibility for customizing your box to suit a special person or unique situation.

Building this project as a gift will showcase your thoughtfulness as well as your woodworking skill.

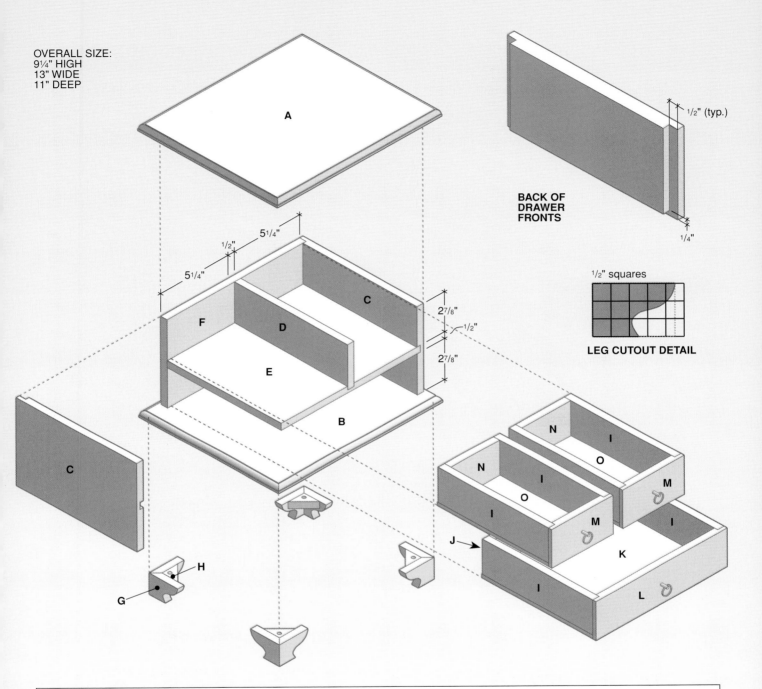

OVERALL SIZE:
9¼" HIGH
13" WIDE
11" DEEP

BACK OF
DRAWER
FRONTS

½" (typ.)

¼"

½" squares

LEG CUTOUT DETAIL

A

C

F

D

C

E

B

H

G

N

I

N

I

O

M

O

I

M

J

I

K

I

L

Cutting List

Key	Part	Dimension	Pcs.	Material
A	Top	¾ × 11 × 13"	1	MDF
B	Bottom	¾ × 11 × 13"	1	MDF
C	Side	½ × 6¼ × 9½"	2	Birch ply.
D	Divider	½ × 3⅛ × 9"	1	Birch ply.
E	Shelf	½ × 9 × 11"	1	Birch ply.
F	Back	½ × 6¼ × 11"	1	Birch ply.
G	Leg	½ × 1½ × 2¼"	8	Birch ply.
H	Glueblock	½ × 1¼ × 1¼"	4	Birch ply.

Cutting List

Key	Part	Dimension	Pcs.	Material
I	Drawer side	½ × 2½ × 8¹¹⁄₁₆"	6	Birch ply.
J	Long drwr. back	½ × 2½ × 9⅜"	1	Birch ply.
K	Long drwr. bottom	¼ × 8¾ × 10⅜"	1	Hardboard
L	Long drwr. front	½ × 2¾ × 10⅜"	1	Birch ply.
M	Short drwr. front	½ × 2¾ × 4⅞"	2	Birch ply.
N	Short drwr. back	½ × 2½ × 3⅞"	2	Birch ply.
O	Short drwr. bottom	¼ × 4⅞ × 8¾"	2	Hardboard

Materials: Wood glue, brads, 4d finish nails, #6 × 1" screws, drawer pulls (3), finishing materials.

Note: Measurements reflect the actual thickness of dimensional lumber.

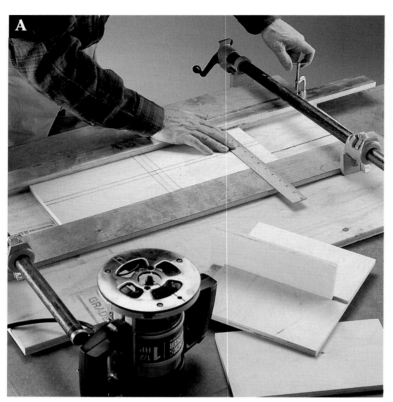

To cut the shelf dadoes, rout both sides in one pass, using a clamped straightedge as a guide for the router base.

Apply glue to the shelf, the divider and the shoulders of the rabbets before attaching the back.

Directions: Jewelry Box

CUT AND SHAPE THE CABINET PARTS. Measure and cut the top (A) and bottom (B) from ¾" MDF. Shape the top edges of both pieces using a router with a ⅜" standard roundover bit.

Measure and cut out the sides (C), divider (D), shelf (E) and back (F). Mark the sides and the shelf for location of dadoes (see *Diagram*), and mark the back edges of the sides for the ½ × ¼"-deep rabbets. To cut the dadoes, clamp the side blanks to your worksurface with back edges butted, clamp a straightedge in place to guide the router base **(photo A),** and use a ½" straight router bit set ¼" deep. Cut the divider dado in the shelf and the back rabbets in the sides using the same process. Drill pilot holes in the dadoes and rabbets.

ASSEMBLE THE CABINET. Attach the divider to the shelf with glue and brads. Stand the shelf/divider assembly on end and attach one side with glue and brads; flip the assembly and attach the other side. Stand the partially assembled cabinet on its front and attach the back with glue and brads **(photo B).** Next, attach the top by centering it on the assembly, drilling pilot holes, and fastening with glue and 4d finish nails. Flip the cabinet over and attach the bottom in the same manner.

MAKE AND ATTACH THE LEGS. Cut four blanks, 6" or longer, from ½ × 1½" stock. Transfer the leg profile (see *Diagram*) to the ends of the blanks and cut the profiles with a jig saw. Clamp the blanks together and gang-sand the cut edges with a drum sander mounted in your drill. Using a power miter box, cut the legs (G) to length, mitering the ends at 45° **(photo C).** Make sure to cut four *pairs* rather than eight identical pieces. Cut the glueblocks (H) to size from ½" scrap.

Assemble the legs by gluing them in pairs to the glueblocks

TIP

Dadoes and rabbets provide strength by increasing the surface area of glue joints and locking components in their proper positions. When machining is done correctly, assembly is almost foolproof. However, accuracy and precision are critical to success, so care invested "up front" will yield dividends later in the process.

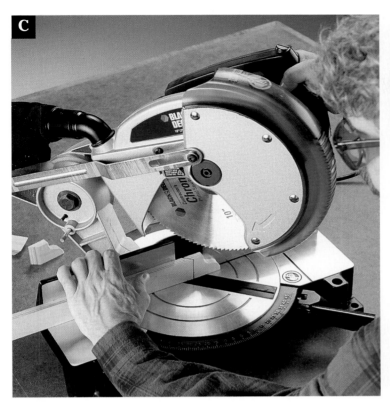

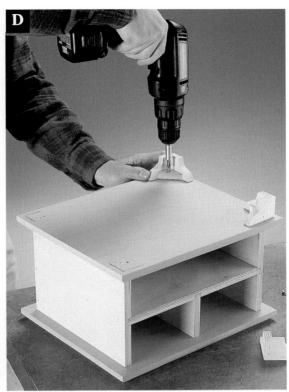

After the leg blanks have been profiled and sanded, cut the leg pieces to length with a power miter box.

Attach the legs with screws and glue, leaving a ⅜" overhang along both sides.

and clamping the pieces with masking tape. After the glue dries, position the legs on the cabinet bottom, drill pilot holes and attach with glue and 1" screws **(photo D).**

BUILD THE DRAWERS. Start by cutting the drawer faces (L, M) to size. Rabbet the backs of these pieces to accept the ½" drawer sides and ¼" bottoms (see *Diagram*). Cut the drawer sides (I) and drawer backs (J, N) to size. Drill pilot holes and assemble the drawer boxes with glue and brads. Cut the drawer bottoms (K) and (O) to size from ¼" hardboard and fasten with glue and brads **(photo E).** Measure and drill for the drawer pulls.

APPLY FINISHING TOUCHES. Set all nail heads, and fill voids with putty. Finish-sand the project, finish as desired and install drawer pulls.

Attach the drawer bottoms with glue and brads. The bottoms hold the drawers square so they fit within their compartments.

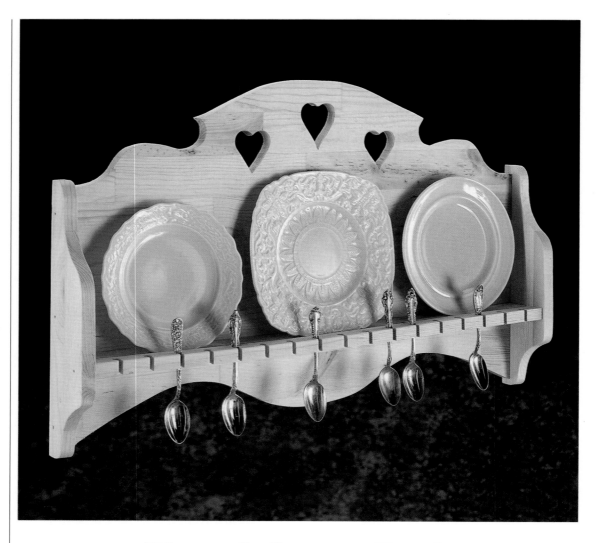

Plate & Spoon Rack

This easy-to-build rack displays your collectibles and shows off your woodworking ability.

CONSTRUCTION MATERIALS

Quantity	Lumber
1	$2^{1}\!/_{32} \times 24 \times 47^{1}\!/_{2}$" ponderosa pine panel

This decorative fixture, made from edge-glued ponderosa pine panels, has features you'll appreciate as your collection continues to grow. The back features three heart cutouts, and scallops along the top edge accentuate your most prized plates. The plate shelf has a groove cut into it to help stabilize up to three full-size plates, while the sides are curved to soften the edges and to better display the plates. The spoon rack sits in front of a curved background that adds interest to the unit, while the rack itself has notches that hold up to seventeen collectible teaspoons in full view.

OVERALL SIZE:
18" HIGH
3⅝" WIDE
27¹³⁄₁₆" LONG

1" squares

SIDE VIEW

4¼"

12½"

PART A DETAIL

1³⁄₈"

¼"

3/8"

1¹⁄₈"   1¹⁄₄" (typ.)   1½" (typ.)   ³⁄₁₆" (typ.)

7/16"

PART C DETAIL

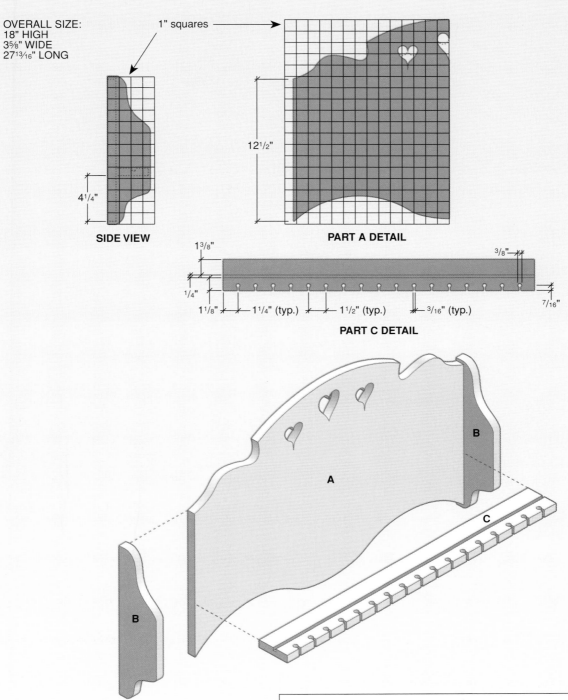

B

A

C

B

Cutting List

Key	Part	Dimension	Pcs.	Material
A	Back	²¹⁄₃₂ × 18 × 26½"	1	Pine panel
B	Side	²¹⁄₃₂ × 3⅝ × 13"	2	Pine panel
C	Shelf	²¹⁄₃₂ × 2¾ × 26½"	1	Pine panel

Materials: #6 × 1½" wood screws, 4d finish nails, 2 steel keyhole hanger plates.

Note: Measurements reflect the actual thickness of dimensional lumber.

Lay out the pattern on the back piece by tracing half the pattern on one side of the centerline, then flipping the pattern and tracing the other side.

Clamp the back to your worksurface, and cut the pattern, using a jig saw.

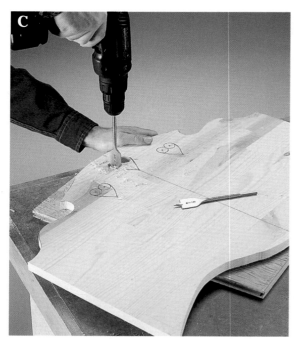

Drill out the larger heart using a 1" spade bit. Use a ⅞" spade bit to create the smaller hearts.

Directions: Plate & Spoon Rack

CUT THE BACK. Laying out the back requires the use of a pattern (see *Diagram*). Our pattern includes half of the back design, and will be flipped to mark two symmetrical halves. Cut the back blank (A) to overall size. Transfer the decorative profile onto cardboard or heavy paper (see *Diagram*). Locate the back piece centerline and work both ways, tracing the pattern on one side of the centerline, then flipping the pattern over at the centerline and tracing the other symmetrical side **(photo A).** Cut the edge shapes with a jig saw, taking care that the ends, which will be attached to the sides, are finished at 12½" **(photo B).**

CUT THE HEART DETAILS. The back has two different-sized heart cutouts (see *Diagram*). Trace these heart cutouts onto the back piece. Place a piece of scrap under the workpiece to protect your worksurface, and start by drilling two horizontally adjacent holes, using a 1" spade bit for the larger heart and a ⅞" bit for the smaller hearts **(photo C)**. Complete the cutouts with a jig saw.

CUT THE SIDES. Cut the sides (B) by transferring the side profile to cardboard (see *Diagram*) and then tracing onto pine. Cut one side with a jig saw, then use the completed side as a pattern to mark and cut the other side.

CUT THE SHELF. The shelf has a groove to hold the plates, and notches to hold the spoons.

Cut the plate groove into the shelf, using bar clamps and a straight-edge to hold the shelf in place and guide the router.

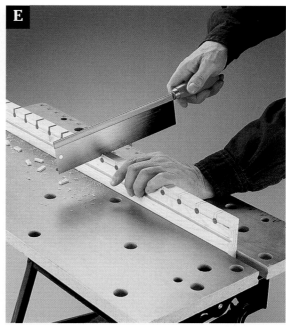

Cut a ³⁄₁₆"-wide notch along the front edge for each of the spoon rack holes, using a backsaw.

First cut the shelf (C) to size. Then cut the groove into the shelf, using a simple routing jig to help make a uniform, straight cut. To make the jig, clamp two pieces of ¾" scrap wood against the edges of the shelf. Securely clamp a straight-edge over the scrap wood to guide the router base and cut the groove at the desired location (see *Diagram*) with a ¼" straight router bit set ¼" deep **(photo D).** Next, measure and mark the 17 spoon hole center-points (see *Diagram*). Drill the holes, using a ⅜" bit. Complete the spoon hole cutouts, using a backsaw to cut straight into the holes, leaving a ³⁄₁₆" slot **(photo E).** Sand all cut edges before assembling.

ASSEMBLE THE RACK. Drill pilot holes into the sides and attach to the back using glue and 4d finish nails. Position the shelf, then drive 4d finish nails through the sides into the shelf

(photo F). Next, drill counter-sunk pilot holes and drive wood screws through the back into the shelf.

APPLY FINISHING TOUCHES. Sand smooth and apply a finish. We recommend amber shellac, which provides a hard, cleanable surface and gives the wood a very warm, rich and even color.

HANG THE RACK. Drill or chisel out space so the keyhole hanger plates are flush with the back surface of the rack. Drive screws through the hanger plates into the back of the rack.

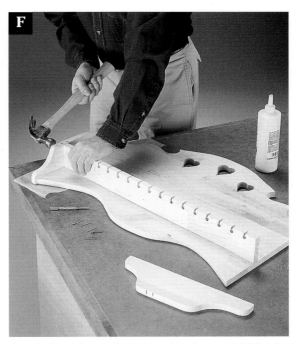

Attach the sides to the back with glue and 4d finish nails, then attach the shelf to the sides with finish nails and to the back with wood screws.

Collector's Table

Store your fine collectibles in this eye-catching conversation piece.

CONSTRUCTION MATERIALS

Quantity	Lumber
1	½" × 4 × 4' oak plywood
1	½" × 4 × 8' oak plywood
1	⅜" × 2 × 2' oak plywood
2	1 × 2" × 6' oak
4	1 × 3" × 8' oak
2	1 × 4" × 6' oak
1	2 × 2" × 6' oak
3	½ × ½ × 30" scrap wood
1	¼ × 18¾ × 34¾" tempered glass

This beautiful, glass-topped collector's table is perfect for storing and displaying shells, rocks, fossils, figurines or other collectibles. It has three interchangeable drawers, so you can change the display whenever you choose—simply by rotating a different drawer into the top position under the glass.

Built from oak and oak plywood, this table gives you the opportunity to demonstrate sophisticated woodworking skills.

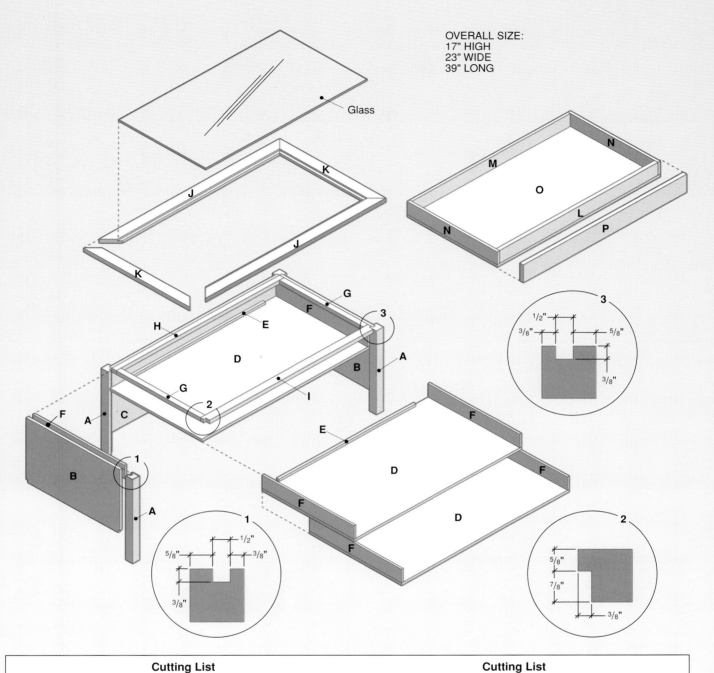

OVERALL SIZE:
17" HIGH
23" WIDE
39" LONG

Cutting List

Key	Part	Dimension	Pcs.	Material
A	Leg	1½ × 1½ × 16¼"	4	Oak
B	End panel	½ × 20¼ × 12½"	2	Oak ply.
C	Back panel	½ × 36¼ × 12½"	1	Oak ply.
D	Shelf	½ × 19⅞ × 36¼"	3	Oak ply.
E	Drawer stop	½ × ½ × 30"	3	Scrap wood
F	Drawer guide	⅜ × 3⅛ × 19⅞"	6	Oak ply.
G	End cleat	¾ × 1 × 18¼"	2	Oak
H	Back cleat	¾ × 1 × 36¼"	1	Oak
I	Top rail	¾ × 1½ × 36¼"	1	Oak
J	Frame, long side	¾ × 2½ × 39"	2	Oak
K	Frame, short side	¾ × 2½ × 23"	2	Oak
L	Drawer box front	¾ × 2½ × 34¼"	3	Oak
M	Drawer box back	½ × 2½ × 34¼"	3	Oak ply.
N	Drawer box side	½ × 2½ × 19½"	6	Oak ply.
O	Drawer bottom	½ × 19½ × 35¼"	3	Plywood
P	Drawer face	¾ × 3½ × 35¼"	3	Oak

Materials: Wood glue, wood screws (1", 1¼"), ⅝" brads, 4d finish nails, finishing materials.

Note: Measurements reflect the actual thickness of dimensional lumber.

Directions: Collector's Table

CUT THE LEGS. It is important to distinguish between the left and right legs when building this table. Each pair of front and back legs has a stopped dado to hold the end panel in place. The back legs also have a second stopped dado to support the back panel (see *Detail*). We recommend you use a router table to make these cuts.

Start by cutting the legs (A) to length. Measure and mark 12"-long dadoes on the legs. On the front legs, cut the dadoes on one face, using a ½" straight bit set to ⅜" depth. On the back legs, cut dadoes on two adjacent faces **(photo A).** Remove the waste section between the back leg dadoes with a saw and square off the dado ends, using a ½" chisel.

CUT PANELS AND ATTACH THE LEGS. Cut the end panels (B) and back panel (C) to size. Cut a ⅜ × ½" notch (see *Detail*) into the bottom corner of each panel **(photo B).** At-

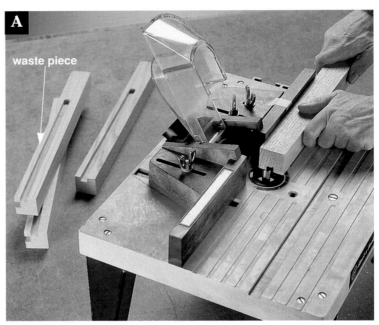

Cut ½ × ⅜"-deep stopped dadoes in the legs, using a router table. Note the waste pieces on the back legs, which you will need to remove with a handsaw and chisel.

Cut a ⅜ × ½" notch out of the bottom corners of the back and side panels where they will overhang the dadoes in the legs.

tach a pair of legs to each end panel, using glue and brads. Set aside the back panel for attachment later.

CUT THE SHELVES, DRAWER STOPS AND DRAWER GUIDES. Because the drawer stops are hidden, they can be built from any scrap ½" lumber.

Cut shelves (D), drawer stops (E) and drawer guides (F) to size. Attach the stops to the shelves with glue and brads (see *Diagram*).

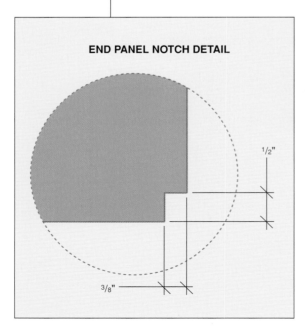

END PANEL NOTCH DETAIL

1/2"

3/8"

Drill pilot holes and attach the bottom drawer guides to the end panel sides, using wood glue and ⅝" brads.

ASSEMBLE THE CABINET. Precision is crucial when assembling your collector's table. Sloppy construction will make it difficult to fit the drawers into the cabinet.

Attach the lowest drawer guides to the inside of the end panels by measuring up from the bottom edge and marking a line at 1¹⁄₁₆". Position the bottom edge of the drawer guide on this line and attach with glue and brads **(photo C).**

Next, attach the back to the side assemblies by setting the back panel into the dadoes on the back legs, keeping all top edges flush. Drill pilot holes and secure the back panel with glue and brads.

Carefully turn the cabinet upside down, then drill countersunk pilot holes and attach the bottom shelf to the edge of the drawer guides with 1" wood screws. Turn the cabinet right-side-up and attach the middle shelf to the top edge of the drawer guide with 1" screws.

Rest the center drawer guides on the middle shelf and fasten to the end panels with glue and ¾" screws **(photo D).** Install the top shelf and upper guides in similar fashion.

Cut the cleats (G, H) and top rail (I) to size. Drill counterbored pilot holes and attach flush with the tops of the back and side panels, using wood glue and 1¼" screws (see *Diagram*).

TIP

Cutting stopped dadoes is a precision task. It's a good idea to practice these skills on scrap wood before you attempt this project.

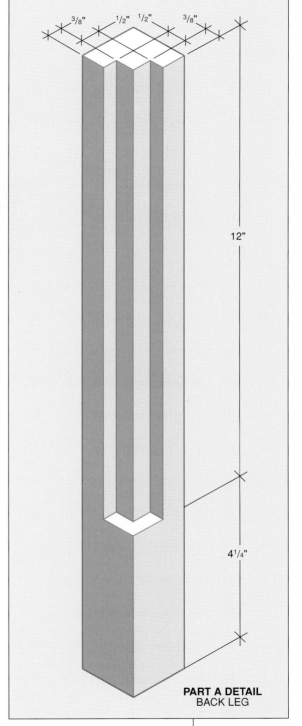

3/8" 1/2" 1/2" 3/8"

12"

4¼"

PART A DETAIL
BACK LEG

Drill countersunk pilot holes and attach the center guides to the end panels, using wood screws.

Glue the miters of the top frame together, using a band clamp. Check for square by measuring diagonals.

BUILD THE TOP FRAME. First cut the long frame sides (J) and short frame sides (K) to length, mitering the ends at 45°. Then cut a rabbet along the inside top edge of the frame pieces, using a router with a ½" straight bit set at ⁵⁄₁₆" depth.

Apply glue to the mitered ends and clamp the frame together, using a band clamp **(photo E).** After the glue has dried thoroughly, center the frame over the cabinet with a

¼" overhang on all sides, drill pilot holes and attach the frame using wood glue and 4d finish nails.

MAKE THE DRAWERS. Cut the drawer box parts (L, M, N, O) to size. Assemble each drawer box by positioning the front

TIP

For easier access to stored collections, you can attach pull knobs to the face of each drawer.

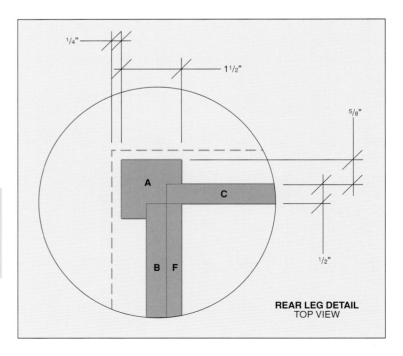

REAR LEG DETAIL
TOP VIEW

Assemble the drawer boxes and attach the bottoms with wood glue and brads. Make sure to check for square as you build each drawer.

Attach drawer faces with glue, and drive wood screws through the inside of the drawer box into the drawer face.

and back between the sides, drilling pilot holes, and attaching the pieces with glue and brads. Make sure drawer assemblies are square. Attach the drawer bottoms, using glue and brads **(photo F).**

Cut the drawer faces (P) to size. Position the drawer faces on the front of the drawer boxes, so the ends are flush and there is a ⁵⁄₁₆" overhang at the top edge and a ³⁄₁₆" overhang at the bottom. Drill pilot holes and attach by driving 1¼" wood screws from inside the drawer box fronts into the drawer face **(photo G).**

Test-fit the completed drawers in the cabinet, making sure there is ⅛" spacing between drawer faces.

FINISH THE CABINET. This project is designed to attract attention, so take care to finish it carefully.

Fill all visible nail holes with putty, then sand all surfaces smooth. Paint the insides and top edges of the drawer boxes (not the drawer faces) with flat black paint to highlight your collectibles. Stain the rest of the wood with a color of your choice (we used a light Danish walnut), and apply several coats of water-based polyurethane finish, sanding lightly between coats.

INSTALL THE GLASS TOP. It's a good idea to wait until the project is built before measuring and ordering the glass for your collector's table. Measure the

length and width of the opening, and reduce each measurement by ⅛". Tempered safety glass is a good choice, especially if you have children. Seat the glass on clear, self-adhesive cushions to dampen any potential rattles.

> ### TIP
>
> *If you wish, the inside of the collection drawers can be lined with black velvet to provide an ultra-elegant setting for your finest collectibles.*

Art Deco Floor Lamp

Twin copper posts create dynamic contrast in this contemporary design.

Add a dash of style to a dark corner of your room with the Art Deco floor lamp. It's a striking addition that's as practical as it is beautiful. The overall design borrows from the long, fluid lines and curves of the Art Deco period, but is deceptively simple in construction. This project combines painted wood, copper tubing and easy-to-find electrical parts to create a singular, modern appeal. The thick half-lap joinery of the base makes an attractive and stable footing for the floor lamp, so accidental tipping won't be a constant worry. The most unusual aspect of the floor lamp is the copper used for the twin columns, made from ordinary water-supply pipe. Surprisingly inexpensive,

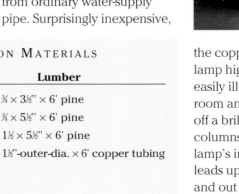

CONSTRUCTION MATERIALS

Quantity	Lumber
1	¾ × 3½" × 6' pine
1	¾ × 5½" × 6' pine
1	1½ × 5½" × 6' pine
2	1½"-outer-dia. × 6' copper tubing

the copper columns raise the lamp high enough so you can easily illuminate an entire room and, when polished, give off a brilliant shine. The columns also conceal the floor lamp's internal wiring, which leads up the base and columns and out through the top, where

you install a lamp hardware kit (available at hardware stores). Various styles of globes or lamp shades can be combined with the floor lamp to complement almost any decor. We used a torchiere-style crystal lamp shade for a broad, warm glow and a contemporary look.

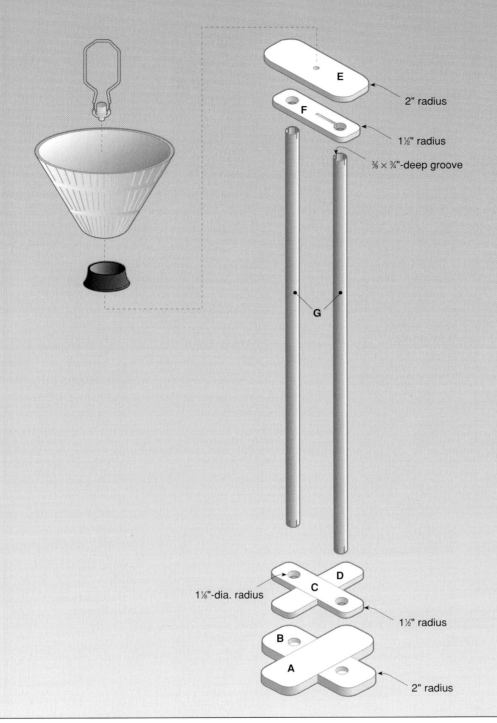

OVERALL SIZE:
60½" HIGH
15" WIDE
15" LONG

E

2" radius

F

1½" radius

⅜ × ¾"-deep groove

G

1⅛"-dia. radius

D

C

1½" radius

B

A

2" radius

Cutting List				
Key	**Part**	**Dimension**	**Pcs.**	**Material**
A	Base bottom	1½ × 5½ × 15"	1	Pine
B	Base side	1½ × 5½ × 4¾"	2	Pine
C	Cross piece	¾ × 3½ × 13"	1	Pine
D	Cross trim	¾ × 3½ × 4¾"	2	Pine

Cutting List				
Key	**Part**	**Dimension**	**Pcs.**	**Material**
E	Lamp seat	¾ × 5½ × 14¼"	1	Pine
F	Seat support	¾ × 3½ × 12¼"	1	Pine
G	Lamp column	1⅛"-dia. × 59½"	2	Copper tube

Materials: Finish nails (3d, 6d), wood glue, #6 × 1¼" wood screws, lamp hardware kit, lamp cord (10' min.), switch, plug, ⅜"-high plastic or rubber feet, wood putty, finishing materials.
Note: Measurements reflect the actual thickness of dimensional lumber.

Directions: Art Deco Floor Lamp

MAKE THE BASE PARTS. The lamp base is made of six rounded boards stacked in a half-lap pattern. Begin by cutting the base bottom (A), base sides (B), cross piece (C) and cross trim (D) to size. On the base bottom, mark lines 2" down and in from each corner, and draw 2"-radius curves at each intersection point. Do the same for two corners on a long edge of each base side. On the cross piece, mark lines 1½"

Drive nails near the ends of the cross piece to secure it to the base bottom and sides.

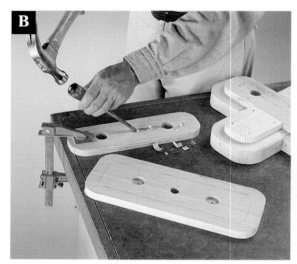

Chisel a groove for the lamp cord into the lamp seat.

down and in from each corner and on two corners on a short edge of the cross trim parts. Draw 1½"-radius curves at these points. Cut the curves with a jig saw, and sand the parts smooth.

ASSEMBLE THE BASE. Draw centerlines on the base bottom and base sides, across their short lengths. Align the base sides on either side of the base bottom so the curves face outward and the centerlines line up. Apply glue to the parts, and toenail them together with 4d finish nails. To help center the cross piece and cross trim, mark several 1"-deep location lines around the outer edges of the base pieces with a combination square or ruler. Center the cross piece over the base parts within the lines, and attach with glue and 6d finish nails **(photo A).** Arrange the cross trim on either side of the cross piece, curves outward and centered within the 1" marks, and attach with glue and finish nails.

MAKE THE LAMP TOP. The top parts are rounded to match the base parts. Cut the lamp seat (E) and seat support (F) to size.

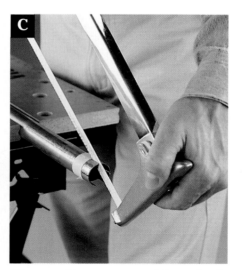

Wrap masking tape around the ends of the lamp columns to mark cutting depth.

Draw 2"-radius curves on the lamp seat corners, and 1½"-radius curves on the seat support corners, using the same method used for shaping the base pieces. Cut the curves with a jig saw, and sand smooth. Drill a ⅛"-dia. hole through the centerpoint of the lamp seat, and mark 1"-long location lines on the lamp seat face around the edges with a combination square. Clamp the seat support onto the lamp seat, centered within the location lines. Flip the clamped parts over, and drive a temporary 1¼" screw through the predrilled center hole, to hold the assembly together for the next step.

CUT COLUMN HOLES. Holes are drilled in the base and top parts for the lamp columns. If you are using alternative material for the lamp columns, such as metal conduit, be sure to measure the actual outside diameter to ensure a proper fit with the respective holes. Adjust the hole diameter, if necessary. Mark centerlines along the length of the cross piece and the seat support. Find the midpoint of each line, and make two marks 4⅛" from either side of the midpoint along the line. Use a 1⅛" spade bit to drill holes centered on these marks, 2" deep on the cross piece and 1½" deep on the seat support.

MAKE CORD PATHS. Holes and grooves on the base and top pieces allow the lamp cord to thread internally through the floor lamp (see *Diagram*, page 37 for additional reference). Disassemble the top parts and drill a

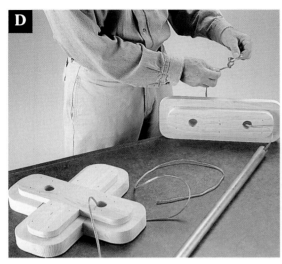

Tie a knot at each end of the lamp cord so it does not become unthreaded.

Use a piece of wood scrap to protect the surface of the lamp seat when securing it to the columns.

¾"-dia. hole through the lamp seat where the ⅛" hole is, to allow the lamp cord to pass to the lamp itself. On the seat support, chisel a ⅜"-dia. × ⅜"-deep groove, from the hole the screw left to one of the 1⅛" holes **(photo B)**. The lamp cord will travel from the column to the lamp in this groove. With the groove facing the lamp seat, center the seat support back on the lamp seat and join the parts with glue and 4d finish nails. On the base parts, center and drill a ¾" hole completely through one of the 1⅛" holes so the lamp cord can exit the floor lamp.

MAKE THE LAMP COLUMNS. The copper lamp columns, made of rigid water-supply tubing, house the lamp cord. Slots are cut into the ends of the columns to aid assembly. Cut the lamp columns (G), using a tubing cutter or a hacksaw with a new blade. Designate top and bottom ends of the lamp columns. On the bottom of each lamp column, cut four 1"-deep slots in an "X"-shape. These slots will help strengthen the epoxy glue bond that secures the copper

tubing. On the top of one of the lamp columns, cut a ⅜"-wide × ¾"-deep groove into one side, to allow the lamp cord to flow into the groove of the seat support. Cut ¾"-deep slots in an "X"-shape in the tops of the lamp columns, including the end with the groove **(photo C)**. Push one end of the lamp cord through the ¾"-dia. hole at the top of the lamp seat, and pull it out through the 1⅛"-dia. hole in the seat support. Feed the lamp cord through the lamp column with the ¾" groove, and run the cord out through the ¾"-dia. hole in the base assembly **(photo D)**.

ATTACH THE LAMP COLUMNS. Rotate the corded column in the base until the groove in the top aligns with the grooved channel in the seat support. Make sure the groove is in the proper position before you attach the lamp columns to the base. Once you've determined the proper position, coat the holes in the base assembly with long-set epoxy (recommended for joining incongruous materials like metal and wood). Let the long-set epoxy set for at

least one hour, and then drive the lamp columns into the holes. Use a wood mallet or a piece of softwood to keep from bending the lamp columns. Be sure that the columns stay straight and perpendicular. When the glue has set, coat the holes in the seat support with epoxy, let set, and then drive the top assembly onto the lamp columns **(photo E)**.

APPLY FINISHING TOUCHES. Let the epoxy dry completely. Fill all holes and gaps with wood putty, and sand all surfaces smooth. Apply primer and paint to the base and top, and allow to dry. Attach a switch and plug to the lamp cord near the base, and install your lamp hardware kit according to the manufacturer's instructions. Use copper polish on the columns, or rub them with an abrasive pad and then seal with car wax or paste wax. Or you can choose to leave the copper unfinished, and in time it will develop a light, greenish patina. Finally, attach ⅜"-high plastic or rubber feet to the base to allow the lamp cord to freely exit the floor lamp.

Kids' Coat Rack

Kids love using this monkey-topped coat rack, and you'll have fun building it.

CONSTRUCTION MATERIALS

Quantity	Lumber
1	2 × 2" × 4' oak
1	1 × 6" × 2' oak
1	¾" × 2 × 2' birch plywood
1	1 × 3" × 4' oak

This stand is designed to hold eight coats or jackets, but kids will hang almost anything on the shaker pegs, including mittens, scarves, sweaters and pants. The decorative monkey acts as a motivator and reminder that it's more fun to hang your clothes on the stand than throw them on the furniture or floor. The monkey also gives you an opportunity to put your artistic talents to work. This popular stand is easy to construct and takes up little space, so it can fit in an entryway or bedroom with ease.

OVERALL SIZE:
58½" HIGH
16" WIDE
16" DEEP

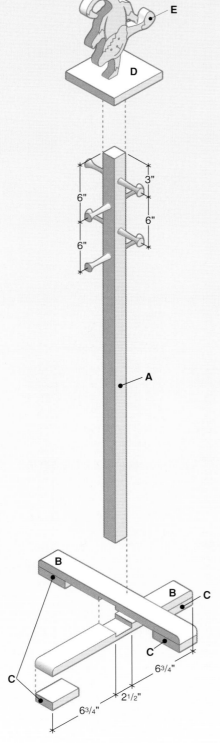

E

D

3"

6"

6"

6"

6"

A

B

B

C

C

C

6¾"

2½"

6¾"

1" squares

CUTOUT DETAIL

	Cutting List			
Key	**Part**	**Dimension**	**Pcs.**	**Material**
A	Post	1½ × 1½ × 46¼"	1	Oak
B	Leg	¾ × 2½ × 16"	2	Oak
C	Foot	¾ × 2½ × 3"	4	Oak
D	Platform	¾ × 5½ × 5½"	1	Oak
E	Monkey	¾ × 8 × 10"	1	Birch plywood

Materials: Wood glue, #8 × 1¼" wood screws,
birch shaker pegs (8), finishing materials.

Note: Measurements reflect the actual thickness
of dimensional lumber.

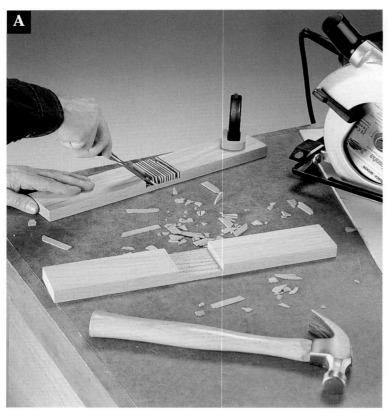

Clean out the half lap joints with a chisel and a hammer. To ensure a tight fit, make sure to keep the edges square.

Mark and drill holes in the post to match the diameter of your shaker pegs.

TIP

To ensure accurate cuts, build a shooting board from a straight piece of 1 × 4" lumber about 24" long, and a smooth piece of ¼"-thick plywood about 6" wide and 24" long. Attach the 1 × 4" board along one edge of the plywood strip, using glue and screws. Then, run your circular saw along the 1 × 4" straightedge, trimming the plywood base to the exact distance between the edge of the saw foot and the blade. To use the shooting board, simply clamp it in place with the edge of the plywood along the cutting line, then run your saw over the plywood with the base of the saw tight against the straightedge.

Directions:
Kids' Coat Rack

CUT THE COAT RACK PARTS. Cut the post (A), legs (B) and feet (C) to length. Align the legs side by side, and clamp together. Mark a 2½"-wide notch on each leg (see *Diagram*). Build a shooting board (see *Tip*), and set the depth of the saw blade at a depth of ⅝" (allowing for the ¼"-thick plywood base, this will give you a ⅜"-deep cut). Clamp the shooting board next to one side of the notch and make the first cut, keeping the saw base flat on the plywood and tight against the straightedge. Repo-

sition the shooting board and cut the other side of the notch. Leave the shooting board in place after the second cut, and make additional cuts within the notch to remove the wood between the first two cuts. Carefully clean any waste from the notch with a sharp ¾" chisel **(photo A).**

Test-fit the legs. If necessary, adjust the lap joint by chiseling, filing or sanding more stock from the notches. Round off the top edges of the leg ends with a router or belt sander.

ASSEMBLE THE PARTS. Glue and clamp the feet to the legs. Position the post on the leg assembly by drawing intersecting

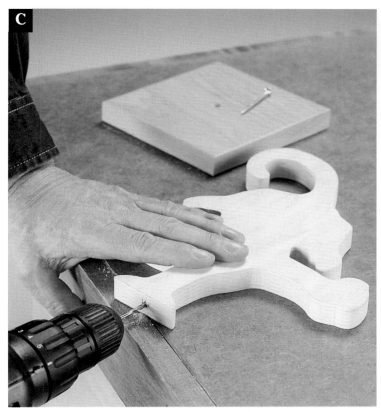

Drill a pilot hole into the base of the monkey so it doesn't split when attaching it to the platform.

Attach the monkey to the platform using glue and a wood screw.

diagonal lines across the notch, then aligning each corner of the post on one of these lines. Drill two countersunk pilot holes through the bottom of the leg assembly, then attach the legs to the post with glue and wood screws.

Mark two peg holes on each side of the post (see *Diagram*). Carefully drill holes straight into the sides of the post, matching the diameter of the shaker pegs **(photo B).**

MAKE THE MONKEY AND PLATFORM. Lay out the monkey pattern (E) on birch plywood (see *Diagram*), and cut out the pattern with a jig saw. Use wood putty to fill any voids on the

edges of the plywood. Cut the platform (D) to size.

Drill a countersunk pilot hole into the bottom of the platform at the centerpoint for attaching the monkey. Drill two offset pilot holes in the top of the platform, about ¾" from the center hole. Counterbore one of these holes. Drill a pilot hole into the center of the monkey's paw **(photo C).** Paint the monkey with brown and white paint.

ASSEMBLE THE UNIT. First attach the monkey to the platform, using glue and a wood screw **(photo D).** Then, attach the monkey and platform to the post assembly with glue, a wood screw and a brad. Attach

> TIP
>
> *For better control when painting faces and figurines, use latex paint as a base coat, and outline the pattern details with a permanent-ink marker. To protect your work, you can seal the monkey with a low-luster water-based polyurethane.*

the shaker pegs with glue, and wipe off any excess.

APPLY THE FINISHING TOUCHES. Sand the project smooth and apply oil or a clear finish.

Two-tier Bookshelf

*Here's a smart-looking, easy-to-build project that has
no glue, screws or nails!*

CONSTRUCTION MATERIALS

Quantity	Lumber
1	¾" × 4 × 8' Baltic birch plywood
1	1"-dia. × 2' birch dowel

This two-tier bookshelf
provides ample room for
encyclopedias, dictio-
naries and other useful
references. The modern side
profile complements many
decorating motifs, and with the
right finish, this project can become a vibrant accent piece.
The bookshelf uses an unusual
joinery method, known as a
pinned mortise-and-tenon, that
requires no glue, screws or
nails in the assembly. Instead,
wedges hold the joints together. When moving or storing
the unit, you can simply remove the wedges.

With the included plan for a
mortising jig, you can easily
make several of these book-
shelves to give as gifts.

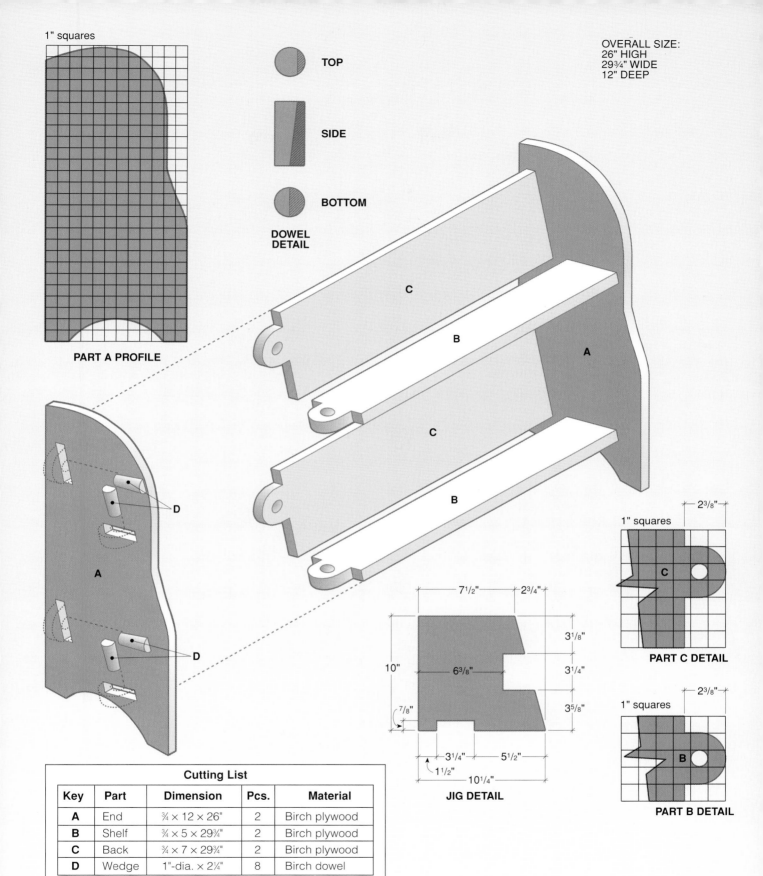

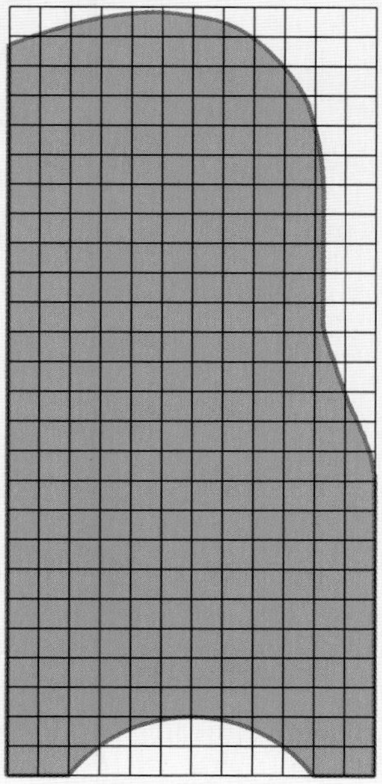
1" squares

PART A PROFILE

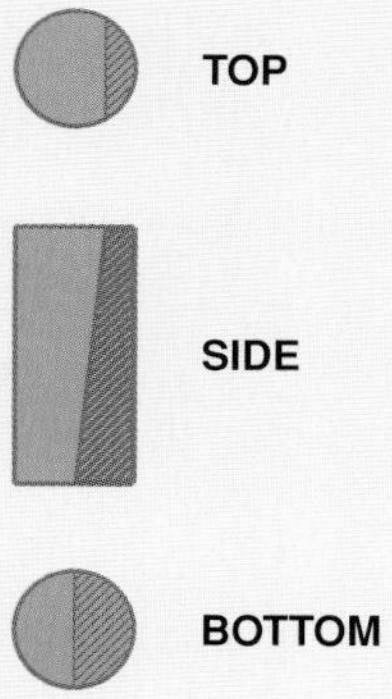
TOP
SIDE
BOTTOM

DOWEL DETAIL

OVERALL SIZE:
26" HIGH
29¾" WIDE
12" DEEP

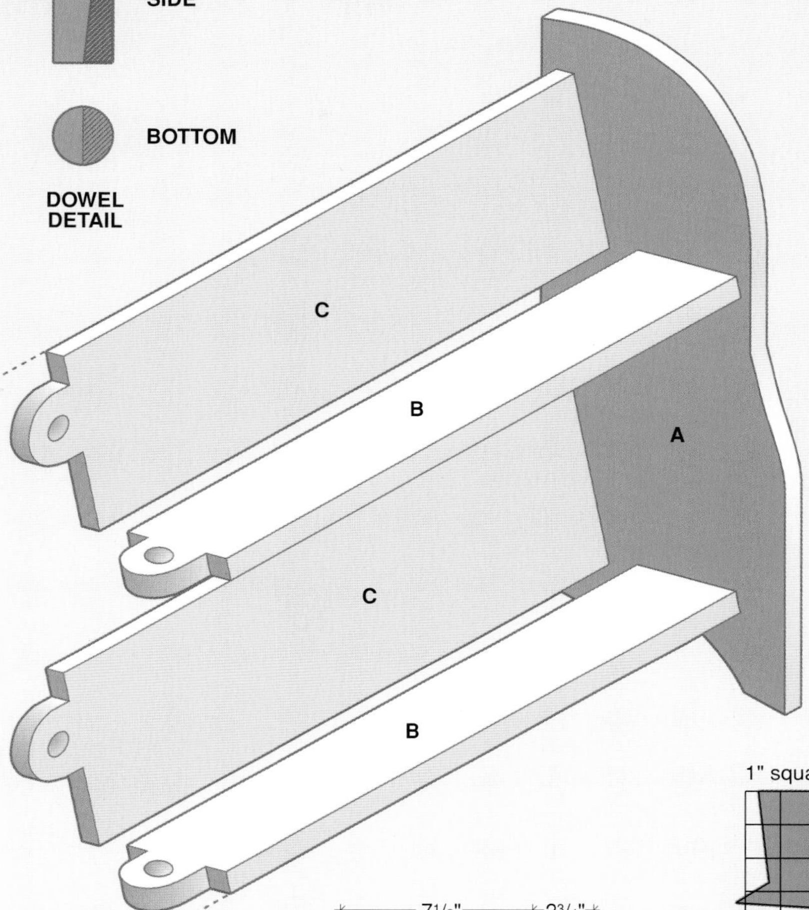
C
B
A
C
B

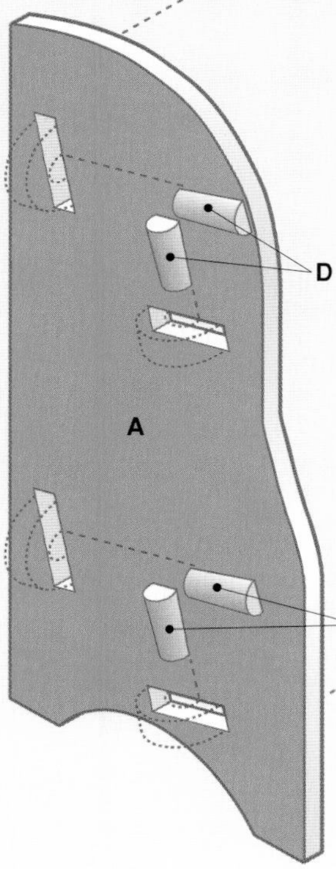
D
A
D

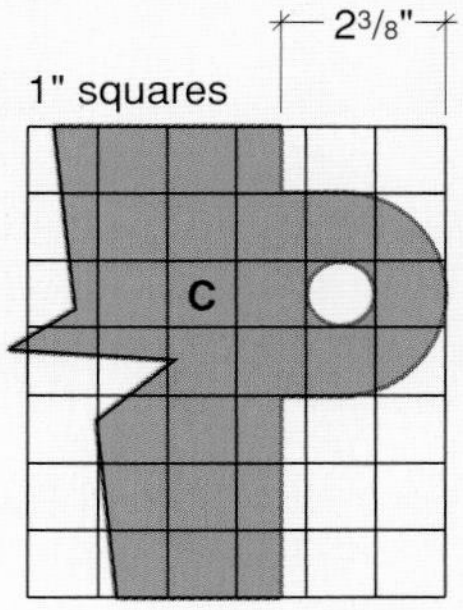
2 3/8"
1" squares
C

PART C DETAIL

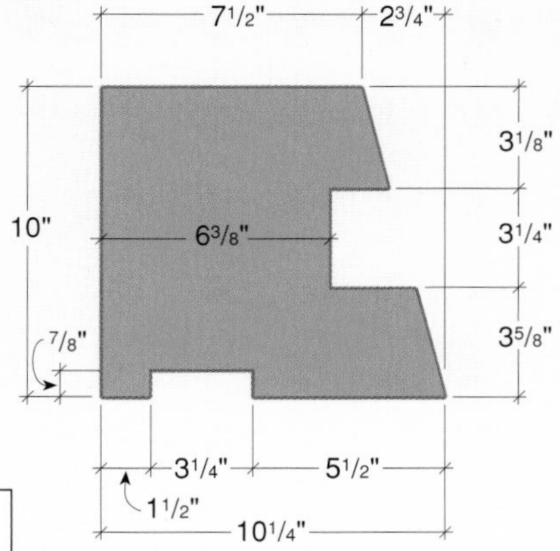
7 1/2"
2 3/4"
3 1/8"
10"
6 3/8"
3 1/4"
3 5/8"
7/8"
3 1/4"
5 1/2"
1 1/2"
10 1/4"

JIG DETAIL

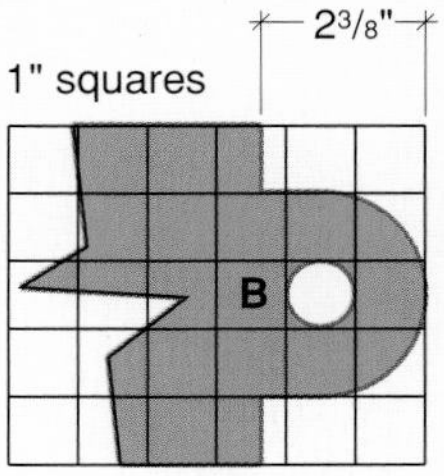
2 3/8"
1" squares
B

PART B DETAIL

Cutting List

Key	Part	Dimension	Pcs.	Material
A	End	¾ × 12 × 26"	2	Birch plywood
B	Shelf	¾ × 5 × 29¾"	2	Birch plywood
C	Back	¾ × 7 × 29¾"	2	Birch plywood
D	Wedge	1"-dia. × 2¼"	8	Birch dowel

Materials: Finishing materials.

Note: Measurements reflect the actual thickness of dimensional lumber.

Directions:
Two-tier Bookshelf

MAKE THE JIG. This project uses a jig to help you accurately mark the location of mortises in the side pieces.

First, cut a 10 × 10¼" blank from ¼" scrap material. Measure and mark the diagonal line and the locations for the mortise guides (see *Diagram*). Use a jig saw to cut out the jig **(photo A)**.

CUT THE ENDS. Cut the end blanks (A) to size, then transfer the pattern (see *Diagram*) and cut with a jig saw. Lay both ends on your workbench with the back edges together, forming a mirror image. Measure from the bottom back corners and mark reference points at ⅞" and 14¾" **(photo B)**.

Lay out the mortises by positioning the bottom back corner of the jig at the first reference point, keeping the back edges flush. Outline the two lower mortises, then slide the jig up to the second reference point and mark the two higher mortises **(photo C)**.

Remove the jig and draw lines to close the ¾ × 3" rectangles. Drill pilot holes and cut out the mortises with your jig saw **(photo D)**.

CUT THE SHELVES AND BACKS. Cut shelves (B) and backs (C) to size. Lay out the profile for the tenons (see *Diagram*) and cut out with a jig saw. Sand the edges smooth. Drill wedge holes, using a 1" spade bit. Test-fit the tenons in the mortises, and make any necessary adjustments.

TIP

To yield an opening large enough to accommodate the tenons, make sure the mortises on your pattern are slightly oversized.

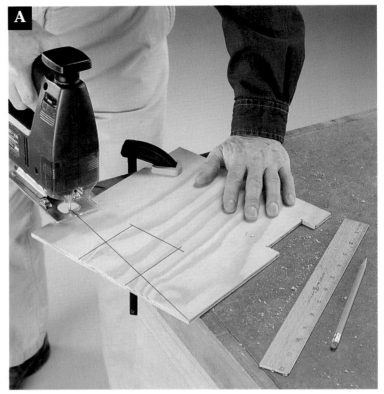

Use a piece of ¼" scrap plywood and your jig saw to create the mortising jig.

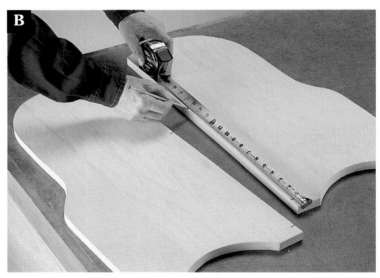

Mark reference points at ⅞" and at 14¾" along the backs of both sides as a guide for positioning the mortise jig.

MAKE THE WEDGES. Create wedges (D) to hold the shelves in place by cutting 1"-dia. dowels to 2¼" lengths. Measure from one edge and mark reference lines across the top of the dowel at ¼" and across the bottom at ½". Connect these lines, then sand the dowels down to this line, using a belt sander clamped horizontally to your worksurface **(photo E)**.

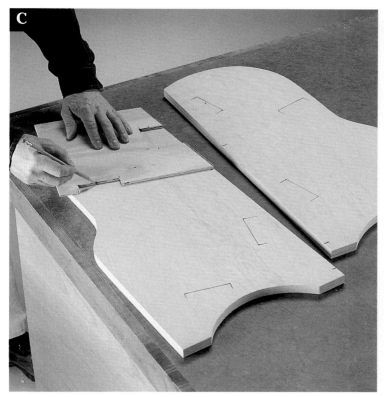

Use the jig to mark the locations of both pairs of mortises, then flip the jig and mark corresponding mortises on the other end piece.

Drill pilot holes and complete the mortises with your jig saw.

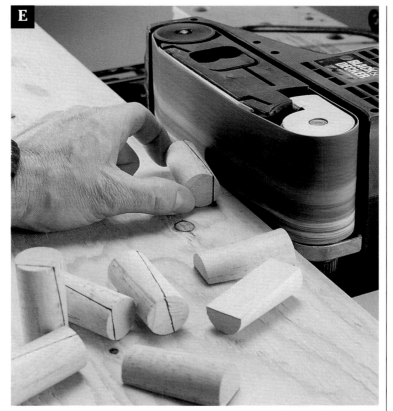

Assemble the shelves and backs between the ends and test-fit the wedges. Disassemble the bookshelf for finishing.

APPLY THE FINISHING TOUCHES. Finish-sand the entire project, then paint or finish the bookshelf as desired. We used a light oil finish, but this project would also be well suited for a bold aniline dye. When the finish dries, assemble the pieces.

Sand the wedges to the lines, using a belt sander clamped to your worksurface.

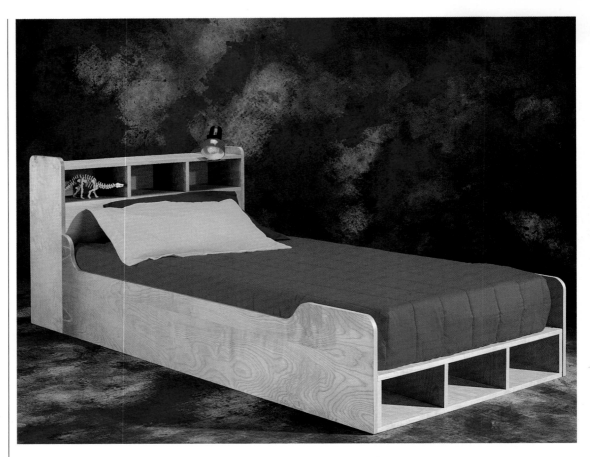

Twin-size Bed Frame

Soft, contemporary lines, warm wood tones, and plenty of built-in storage make this bed frame the centerpiece of any bedroom.

Beds, roller skates and winter coats have one thing in common: your child can outgrow them very quickly. While there is little you can do to make skates and coats last more than one or two seasons, a bed frame is a different story. This attractive bed frame is designed with fun lines and six separate storage compartments, making it an exciting choice for a child's first real bed. But unlike many kids' beds that take fanciful design to an extreme, this bed can serve your child well into his or her teens, without seeming like an overgrown crib. And because it is made from two sheets of plywood, you can build it for a fraction of the cost of a less versatile, cheaply constructed bed that is purchased at a kids' furniture store.

This bed frame is sized to support a standard twin-size box spring and mattress. Be-cause the box spring rests on wood cleats on the sides of the wood panel bedrails, you don't need to purchase any expensive bed rails or other bed hardware to make it. The main panels of the bed frame are connected with metal brackets, so the frame can be disassembled easily for transportation.

An assortment of storage cubbies and handy surfaces are well positioned for a reading lamp and alarm clock, as well as clothing that will not fit into closets or dressers. We chose a natural wood finish for our bed frame, but you can paint yours if you prefer.

CONSTRUCTION MATERIALS

Quantity	Lumber
1	¼" × 4 × 4' AB plywood
1	¾" × 4 × 8' birch plywood
3	2 × 2" × 8' pine

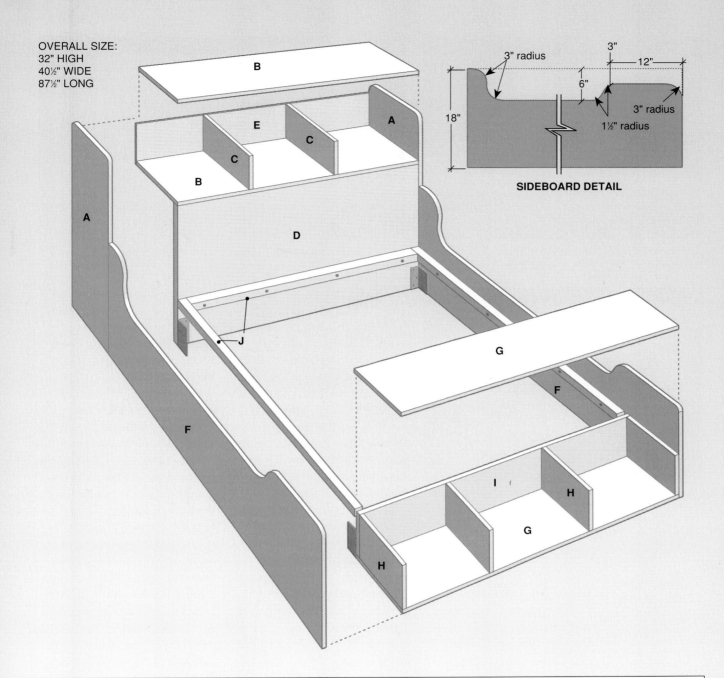

OVERALL SIZE:
32" HIGH
40½" WIDE
87½" LONG

SIDEBOARD DETAIL

3" radius

3"

12"

6"

18"

3" radius

1½" radius

Cutting List

Key	Part	Dimension	Pcs.	Material
A	Side panel	¾ × 11½ × 32"	2	Plywood
B	Headboard shelf	¾ × 11¼ × 39"	2	Plywood
C	Headboard divider	¾ × 11¼ × 6"	2	Plywood
D	Front panel	¾ × 39 × 23"	1	Plywood
E	Headboard back	¼ × 39 × 7¼"	1	Plywood

Cutting List

Key	Part	Dimension	Pcs.	Material
F	Sideboard	¾ × 18 × 76"	2	Plywood
G	Footboard shelf	¾ × 12 × 39"	2	Plywood
H	Footboard divider	¾ × 12 × 6"	4	Plywood
I	Footboard back	¾ × 39 × 7½"	1	Plywood
J	Ledger	1½ × 1½ × *	4	Pine

Materials: Wood glue, #6 × ¾" and 1½" wood screws, 2d finish nails, 1½" corner brackets (4), birch veneer edge tape (50'), ⅜"-dia. birch wood plugs, finishing materials.

Note: Measurements reflect the actual size of dimensional lumber.
* Cut to fit

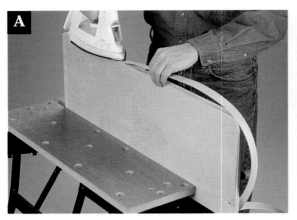

Apply self-adhesive birch veneer edge tape to plywood edges, using a household iron.

Draw a layout line for the bottom shelf across the side panels, even with the top of the front panel.

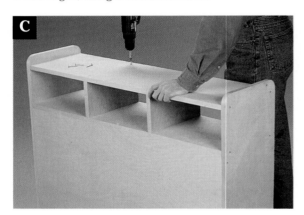

Secure the top shelf to the dividers and side panels with glue and counterbored screws.

Directions:
Twin-size Bed Frame

MAKE THE SIDE PANELS. The side panels form the sides of the headboard unit. We used birch plywood for all plywood parts, but you could substitute oak plywood, or use a good cabinet grade (AB) fir plywood if you plan to paint the bed frame. Cut the side panels (A) to size from ¾"-thick birch plywood, then draw 3"-radius curves at the top corners of the side panels. Cut the curves with a jig saw. Lay one side panel on top of the other panel and trace the curved corners onto the other side panel. Cut the second set of curves. Smooth out the curves with a power

sander and medium-grit sandpaper. Clean the edges of the panels thoroughly, then apply self-adhesive wood veneer edge tape to the edges of both panels. Cut the strips to length, then press them into place with a household iron **(photo A)**—the heat from the iron activates the adhesive. After the tape is set, trim off any veneer overhang with a utility knife, then sand the edges smooth.

MAKE & INSTALL THE FRONT PANEL & SHELVES. The front panel and shelves fit between the side panels to form the headboard. Cut the front panel (D) to size from ¾"-thick birch plywood. Fasten the front panel to the side panels so the bottoms of all panels are flush and the front edges of the side panels are flush with the front face of the front panel. Use glue and #6 × 1½" wood screws. Drive the screws through pilot holes that are counterbored to accept birch wood plugs (usually ⅜" dia.). Cut the headboard shelf (B) and the headboard dividers (C) to size, and smooth the cut edges with a sander. Apply edge tape to the front edges of the parts. Stand the headboard assembly upright and use a square to draw a

reference line across the inside faces of the side panels, even with the top of the front panel **(photo B).** Position the lower headboard shelf on the top edge of the front panel, flush with the reference lines. Drill counterbored pilot holes through the side panels into the ends of the shelf, then fasten the shelf to the side panels with glue and #6 × 1½" wood screws. Measure 13" from each end of the bottom shelf and draw lines across the shelf. Position a headboard divider inside each mark, and secure the dividers with glue and screws driven up through the bottom shelf. Position the upper headboard shelf on the dividers, with the ends of the shelf flush against the inside faces of the side panels. Make sure the dividers are exactly perpendicular to the lower headboard shelf, then fasten them to the upper shelf with glue and counterbored screws **(photo C).** Also drive screws through the side panels and into the ends of the upper headboard shelf. Cut the headboard back (E) to size from ¼"-thick plywood, and fasten it to the back of the headboard with 2d finish nails **(photo D).**

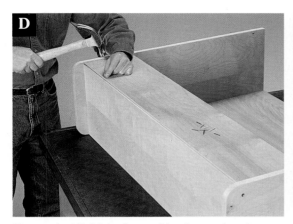

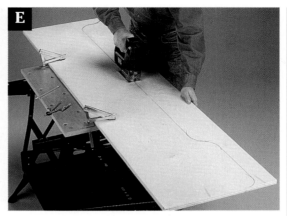

Fasten the ¼"-thick plywood back panel to the headboard using 2d finish nails.

Draw contoured cutting lines on the top edges of the sideboards, then cut with a jig saw.

MAKE THE FOOTBOARD. The footboard is similar to the headboard. Cut the footboard shelves (G) and footboard dividers (H) to size. Apply wood veneer edge tape to the front edges. Draw a reference line 13" from each end of the bottom shelf. Position a footboard divider inside each reference line, and at the ends of the footboard shelves. Secure the dividers with glue and screws driven through the shelves and into the tops and bottoms of the dividers. Make sure the front edges of the parts are flush. Cut the footboard back (I) to size and fasten it to the backs of the shelves and dividers with glue and screws.

BUILD THE SIDEBOARDS. The sideboards connect the headboard to the footboard, while supporting ledgers that hold the box spring. Cut the sideboards (F) to size. Lay out the curves and contours along the top edge (see *Diagram*, page 49) of one sideboard. Cut the top edge of a sideboard to shape with a jig saw **(photo E).** Smooth the edges with a sander, then use the sideboard as a template for tracing a matching contour onto the other sideboard. Cut and sand

the second sideboard, then apply wood veneer edge tape to the top and front edges. Fit the headboard and footboard between the sideboards, so the outside of the footboard is flush with the front ends of the sideboards, and the headboard unit is butted against the back edges of the sideboards. Use duct tape to fasten the parts together temporarily, then check to make sure everything is square. Measure from the front of the headboard to the back of the footboard, and cut two 2 × 2 pine ledgers (J) to this length. Remove the sideboards, and fasten the ledgers to the inside faces so they are 7½" up from the bottoms of the sideboards, flush with the back edges. Use #6 × 1½" screws fastened at 8" intervals to attach the ledgers. Replace the sideboards, and measure between the ledgers on the sideboards to find the right length for the ledgers that are attached to the headboard and footboard. Cut and attach these ledgers, so the tops of all ledgers are flush.

ASSEMBLE THE BED. Attach the headboard and footboard to the sideboards with metal corner-brackets at each joint **(photo F).** Set your twin-size

box spring onto the ledgers to make sure everything fits.

APPLY THE FINISH. Disassemble the frame, then fill all counterbores with wood plugs. Sand the plugs flush with the surfaces, then finish-sand all wood surfaces with 150- to 180-grit sandpaper. Apply stain or paint (we used a light oak stain). Apply finish materials to all wood surfaces. Apply at least two coats of topcoat (we used water-based polyurethane with a satin gloss). Reassemble the bed frame in the room where it will be used.

Fasten the sideboards to the headboard and footboard with corner brackets and screws.

Plate Drying Rack

*This compact plate drying rack is handsome enough to double
as a dinnerware display case.*

The holding capacity and
clean vertical lines of this
plate drying rack could
easily make it a beloved fixture
in your kitchen. The efficient
open design lets air circulate to
dry mugs, bowls and plates
more efficiently than most in-
the-sink types of racks. The rack
is handsome enough to double
as a display rack to showcase
your dinnerware. Even though
it has a small 9¼ × 21½" foot-
print, the rack lets you dry or
store up to 20 full-size dinner
plates plus cups or glasses.
The tall dowels in the back of
the rack are removable so you
can rearrange them to accommodate large or unusually
shaped dishes.

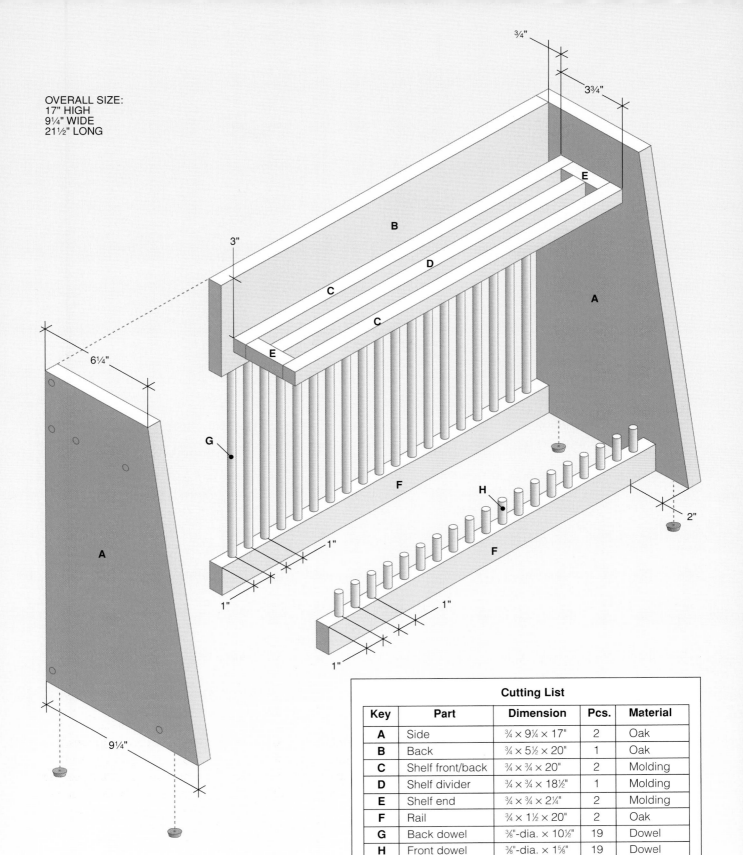

OVERALL SIZE:
17" HIGH
9¼" WIDE
21½" LONG

¾"

3¾"

3"

B

D

E

C

C

A

E

6¼"

A

G

F

H

F

2"

1"

1"

1"

9¼"

1"

Cutting List

Key	Part	Dimension	Pcs.	Material
A	Side	¾ × 9¼ × 17"	2	Oak
B	Back	¾ × 5½ × 20"	1	Oak
C	Shelf front/back	¾ × ¾ × 20"	2	Molding
D	Shelf divider	¾ × ¾ × 18½"	1	Molding
E	Shelf end	¾ × ¾ × 2¼"	2	Molding
F	Rail	¾ × 1½ × 20"	2	Oak
G	Back dowel	⅜"-dia. × 10½"	19	Dowel
H	Front dowel	⅜"-dia. × 1⅝"	19	Dowel

Materials: Waterproof glue, #8 × 1⅝" screws, 4d finish nails,
⅜"-dia. flat oak plugs, rubber feet (4), finishing materials.

Note: Measurements reflect the actual thickness of
dimensional lumber.

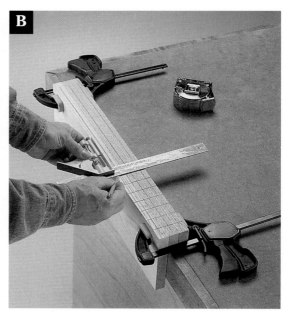

Lay out the sides (A) so they are 9¼" long at the bottom and 6¼" wide at the top.

Speed up measuring the 57 dowel hole locations by clamping the rails and back together.

Directions:
Plate Drying Rack

CUT THE SIDES. The sides have a slight backward slant that gives you easier access to the dishes. This slant requires cutting a diagonal line from the top to the bottom. First, lay out and mark the sides (A) so they are 9¼" long at the bottom and 6¼" wide at the top. Connect these marks, and cut along the diagonal line with a circular saw **(photo A).**

CUT AND DRILL BACK AND RAILS. Cut the back (B) and rails (F) to length, and clamp them together. Measure and mark the dowel holes (see *Diagram*) on the edge of each part **(photo B).** Drill the ¼"-deep dowel holes in the two rails, then re-set the depth of your drill to ½" and drill the deeper dowel holes in the back.

ASSEMBLE SIDES, BACK AND RAILS. Drill ⅜"-dia. counterbored pilot holes through the sides where the back and back rail will be attached. Apply waterproof glue, and attach the pieces with wood screws.

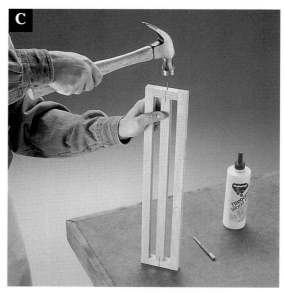

Glue and nail divider in place.

BUILD THE SHELF. Cut the shelf front/back pieces (C), divider (D) and ends (E) to length.

TIP

To make installing the longer 10½" back dowels easier, drill the dowel holes in the back a full ½" deep. When assembling, slide the dowels up into the ½" holes in the back piece and let them drop down into the ¼" holes in the back rail. This lets you easily remove specific dowels to accommodate larger dishes or bowls. Dowel sizes tend to vary so test your dowel sizes by drilling a hole in scrap wood first, using a brad-point bit slightly larger than the ⅜" dowel.

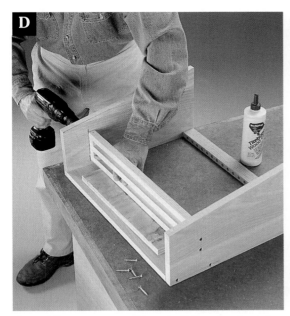

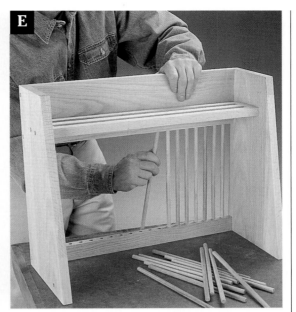

Use a ¾" spacer to position shelf from back while you drill counterbored pilot holes.

Insert dowels into the holes under the back first, then drop them down into the holes in the rail.

Position the shelf front, back and ends together, and drill pilot holes for 4d finish nails. Apply glue, and nail the pieces together. Glue and nail the divider in place **(photo C)**. Next, carefully drill counterbored pilot holes through the sides where the shelf attaches. To properly position the shelf, lay the entire unit on its back. Position the shelf 3" down from the top of the rack, using a ¾"- thick piece of scrap material as a spacer between the shelf and the back. Drill the counterbored pilot holes **(photo D)**. (Be sure to drill the pilot holes into the long shelf pieces and not through the dividers.) Apply glue, and secure the shelf with wood screws.

CUT AND INSERT DOWELS. Cut the back dowels (G) to length. Position these longer dowels by inserting them up the holes in the back, then dropping them down into the back rail **(photo E)**. To complete the front rail (F), cut the front dowels (H) to length. Sand the edges of one end of each dowel. Using waterproof glue, secure the unsanded ends of the front dowels into the front rail holes.

ATTACH THE FRONT RAIL. Position the front rail 2" back from the front edge of the rack, and drill counterbored pilot holes through the sides. Apply waterproof glue, and screw the front rail in place **(photo F)**.

APPLY FINISHING TOUCHES. Fill all counterbored screw holes

with oak plugs. Sand smooth the entire rack and all dowels with 150-grit sandpaper. Apply a water-based polyurethane finish, and attach rubber feet to the bottom of the rack.

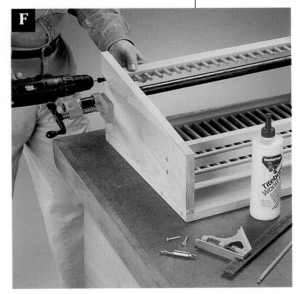

Clamp the front rail, predrill sides, counterbore, glue and screw in place.

TIP

If you plan on consistently using dishes of unusual size, you may choose to change the location of the front rail. The location specified will work well for plates as small as 7" and as large as 11".

Pot Racks

*Turn your kitchen into a space-saving cooking center
with these versatile pot racks.*

CONSTRUCTION MATERIALS

Ladder Rack

Quantity	Lumber
1	1 × 3" × 8' oak
3	1"-dia. × 3' oak dowel

Square Rack

Quantity	Lumber
2	1 × 3" × 8' oak

These inexpensive, easy-to-build oak racks are wonderful pot organizers and great additions to any kitchen, especially if yours suffers from limited cabinet or countertop space. Most busy cooks have one or more overhead racks in their kitchen to keep frequently used cooking items up and out of the way.

Overhead racks also give the proud cook an opportunity to show off copper pans and other gourmet cooking equipment. We've included construction options for a ladder rack with wood dowels, and a larger square rack with lap joints—choose whichever one best suits your kitchen's decor and your personal taste.

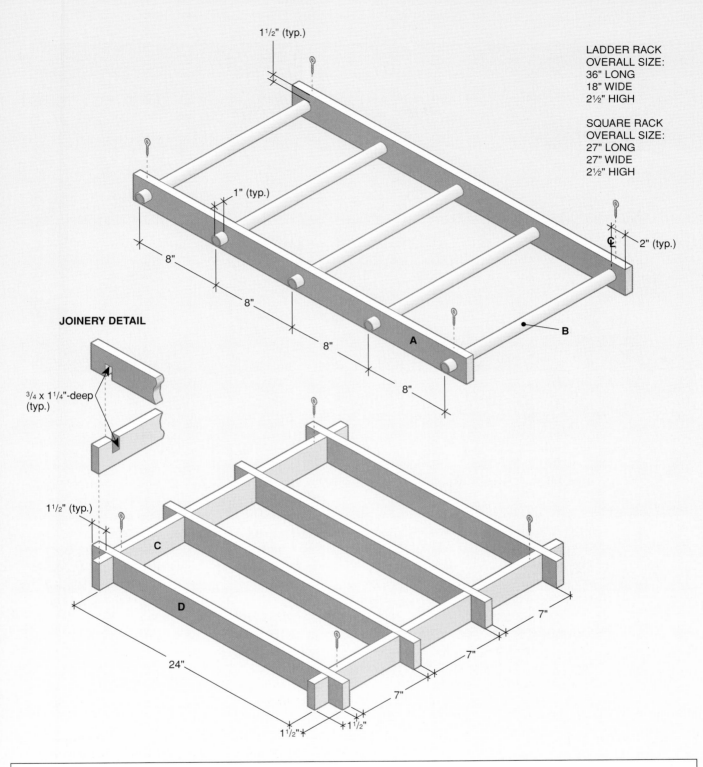

1¹/₂" (typ.)

LADDER RACK
OVERALL SIZE:
36" LONG
18" WIDE
2½" HIGH

SQUARE RACK
OVERALL SIZE:
27" LONG
27" WIDE
2½" HIGH

1" (typ.)

2" (typ.)

8"

8"

C

8"

A

B

8"

JOINERY DETAIL

³/₄ x 1¹/₄"-deep
(typ.)

1¹/₂" (typ.)

C

D

24"

7"

7"

7"

1¹/₂"   1¹/₂"

Ladder Rack Cutting List				
Key	Part	Dimension	Pcs.	Material
A	Stretcher	¾ × 2½ × 36"	2	Oak
B	Dowel	1"-dia. × 18"	5	Dowel

Square Rack Cutting List				
Key	Part	Dimension	Pcs.	Material
C	Rail	¾ × 2½ × 27"	2	Oak
D	Slat	¾ × 2½ × 27"	4	Oak

Materials: Wood glue, 4d finish nails, decorative chain, S-shaped pot hooks, screw eyes (4 for each rack), finishing materials.

Note: Measurements reflect the actual thickness of dimensional lumber.

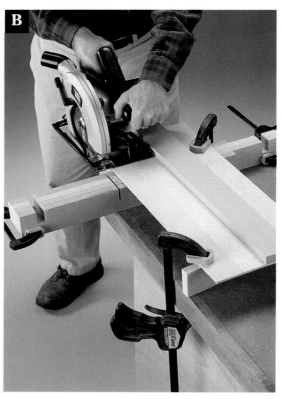

Gang the pieces together and trim the ends with a circular saw and shooting board to remove checks and cracks.

To start the square rack, mark and cut edge lap joints on the rails and slats.

Directions: Square Rack

MAKE A SHOOTING BOARD. A makeshift "shooting board" will help you make clean, accurate cuts across several parts at once. Fasten a 1 × 4 straight-edge, approximately 24" long, to a scrap piece of ¼" plywood. Guide your circular saw against one side of the straightedge to trim the plywood parallel. The shooting board holds ganged parts together, and provides a straight, flat guide for more accurate cutting.

CUT THE PARTS. Cut the rails (C) and slats (D) roughly to size. Align the rails and slats, clamp together and trim to length using the shooting board and your circular saw to remove checks and cracks **(photo A).**

NOTCH THE LAP JOINTS. Lay out 4 notches on each rail and 2 notches on each slat for the lap joints. Make notches ¾" wide × 1¼" deep (see *Diagram* for placement). To make uniform cuts, clamp like pieces together—rail with rail and slat with slat—so the joint notches align. Set the depth of the saw blade at exactly 1½" to allow for both the desired depth of cut and the ¼" plywood of the shooting board. Clamp the shooting board in place next to one edge of the notch, and make the cut, keeping your saw flat on the plywood and

tight to the straightedge. Reposition the shooting board, and cut the other side of the notch **(photo B).** Check that the distance between the outside of these defining cuts is ¾". Leave the shooting board in place after the second cut, and, keeping your saw flat on the ¼" plywood, make additional cuts to remove the wood between the first two cuts. Clean any waste from the notch with a sharp ¾" chisel to ensure tight-fitting joints. Repeat this process for all the notches **(photo C).** Take care not to damage the joint edges.

ASSEMBLE THE RACK. Test-fit the rails and slats. Make any adjustments in the lap joints by chiseling, filing or sanding out more stock in the notch. Glue, assemble and finish-nail the square rack together.

Chisel out debris from lap joints to ensure a good, tight fit.

Place a scrap of plywood under the stretchers to prevent tearouts, and to protect your worksurface.

APPLY FINISHING TOUCHES. Sand the rack smooth and apply a water-based polyurethane finish. Drill pilot holes in the slats, if necessary, and attach pot hooks you've purchased from a hardware store. Thread four screw eyes into the tops of the rails (see *Diagram*). Attach chains to rack, and secure to the ceiling joists with additional screw eyes.

Directions: Ladder Rack

CUT AND DRILL THE STRETCHERS. The stretchers hold the dowels in place and create the outside frame. Trim the stretchers (A) to length with your circular saw and the shooting board, keeping your saw flat on the shooting board and the sole of the saw tight to the guide **(photo A)**. Mark the dowel locations on one stretcher (see *Diagram*). Clamp the stretchers together and drill 1" holes using your power drill equipped with a drill guide **(photo D)**.

PREPARE THE DOWELS. Double-check that your dowels fit through the holes you're drilling. Cut the dowels (B) to 18" lengths, and, if needed, bevel the ends with a power sander until they fit their respective holes.

ASSEMBLE THE RACK. Secure dowels to the stretchers by drilling 1/16" pilot holes through the top edges of the stretchers. Drill all the way into the 1"-dia. dowel holes. Position the dowels so they extend 1" past the stretchers, glue and fasten in place with 4d finishing nails **(photo E)**.

APPLY FINISHING TOUCHES. Sand smooth and apply a water-based polyurethane fin-

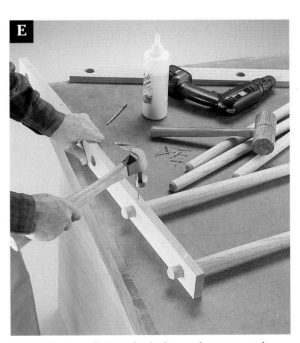

Insert the dowels into the holes and secure each with a 4d finish nail.

ish. Attach chains in the same fashion used with the square rack, and secure to ceiling joists with screw eyes.

Vegetable Bin

Whether your vegetables come from the garden or the grocer, our oak bin keeps them organized and out of the way.

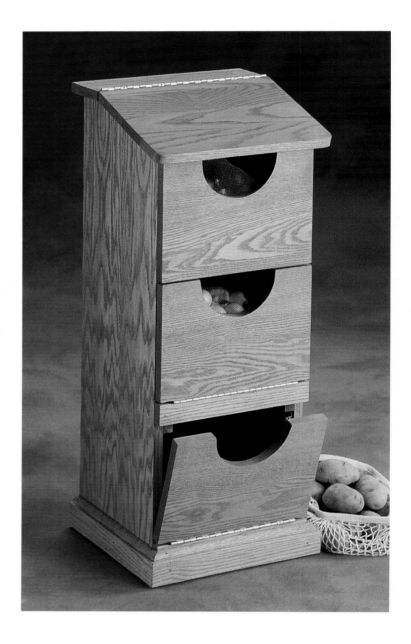

CONSTRUCTION MATERIALS

Quantity	Lumber
1	¾" × 4 × 4' oak plywood
1	¾ × 1½" × 4' oak
1	¾ × 11¼" × 6' oak
1	½ × ½" × 4' quarter-round molding

Not all foods require immediate refrigeration. Onions, potatoes, garlic, shallots and avocados are just some of the foods that don't need to take up precious refrigerator space. But when countertop real estate is also at a premium, veggies often clutter up needed table space or remain in paper bags. Our vegetable bin provides a beautiful, spacious alternative for storing fresh vegetables and fruits. Three separate sections, with hinged bin faces on the sides and top, keep vegetables apart and in place, and make access easy. The sturdy oak construction also provides protection for more fragile items, so your prize tomatoes can stay safely in the shade. The bin's compact vertical design doesn't take up acres of space (just over a square foot), and the rich oak finish trim guarantees a handsome addition to any country (or city) kitchen.

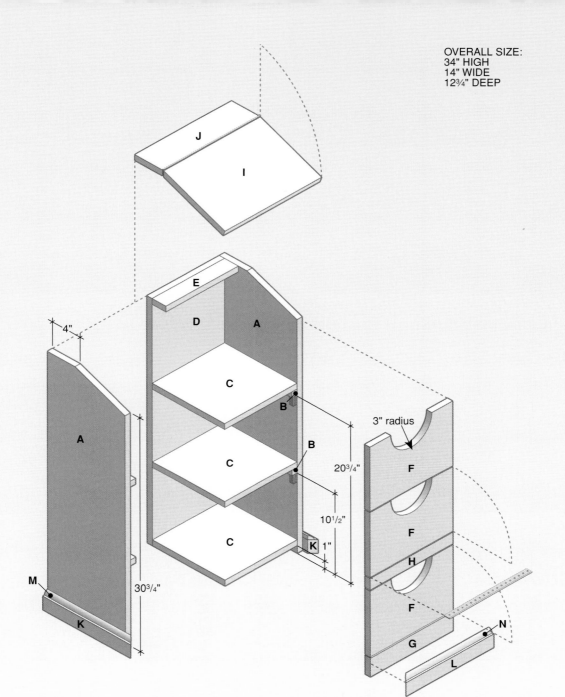

OVERALL SIZE:
34" HIGH
14" WIDE
12¾" DEEP

4"

J

I

E

D   A

C

B

B

3" radius

F

A

20¾"

F

10½"

H

K   1"

F

M

30¾"

K

G

L

N

Cutting List

Key	Part	Dimension	Pcs.	Material
A	Side panel	¾ × 11¼ × 33¼"	2	Plywood
B	Shelf cleat	¾ × ¾ × 10½"	4	Oak
C	Shelf	¾ × 10½ × 10½"	3	Plywood
D	Back	¾ × 10½ × 32¼"	1	Plywood
E	Top cleat	¾ × 2 × 10½"	1	Plywood
F	Bin face	¾ × 8½ × 12"	3	Oak
G	Lower rail	¾ × 2½ × 12"	1	Oak

Cutting List

Key	Part	Dimension	Pcs.	Material
H	Upper rail	¾ × 1½ × 12"	1	Oak
I	Lid	¾ × 9½ × 14"	1	Oak
J	Fixed top	¾ × 4 × 14"	1	Oak
K	Base trim side	¾ × 1½ × 12¾"	2	Oak
L	Base trim front	¾ × 1½ × 13½"	1	Oak
M	Quarter-round side	½ × ½ × 12½"	2	Molding
N	Quarter-round front	½ × ½ × 13"	1	Molding

Materials: Wood glue, oak-veneer edge tape (20'), #6 × 1¼" wood screws, wire brads (1¼", 1½"), 1½" × 36" piano hinge, magnetic door catches (2), chain stops (2), finishing materials.

Note: Measurements reflect the actual thickness of dimensional lumber.

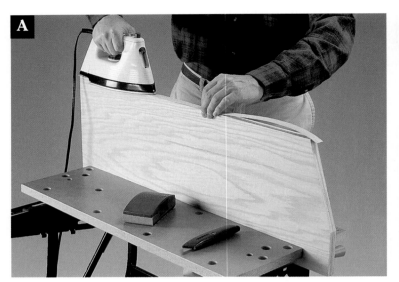

Apply oak-veneer edge tape with a household iron, and trim with a utility knife when cool.

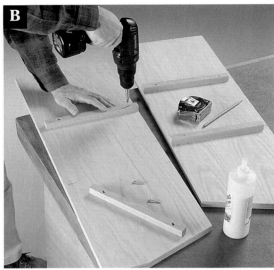

Align cleats on the reference lines, and fasten with glue and screws.

Directions: Vegetable Bin

Use a nail set to recess nail heads flush with the shelves.

MAKE THE SIDES. Cut the side panels (A), shelves (C), back (D) and top cleat (E) to size from plywood, and rip the shelf cleats (B) to size from 1 × 12 oak. Sand all edges smooth. Draw a cutline for the front corners on each side panel (see *Diagram*), and cut along the line with a jig saw to shape the side panels. Clamp each side panel in an upright position, and apply oak-veneer edge tape to all edges using a household iron **(photo A).** Let the veneer cool, and trim the edges with a utility knife. Measure and mark cleat and shelf locations across the inner face of each panel, 1", 10½" and 20¾" from the bottom. Drill countersink pilot holes, then use glue and screws to attach the cleats to the side panels **(photo B).** The bottom of the cleats should be flush with the marked lines, and the front of the cleats should be flush with the front edges of the side panels.

ATTACH THE SIDES AND BACK. Position the bottom shelf between the side panels so the bottom edge of the shelf rests on the 1" reference line. Keep the front edge flush with the side panels, and fasten with glue and screws. Attach the remaining shelves to the cleats with glue and 1¼" brads, using a nail set to recess the nail heads **(photo C).** Use glue and screws to attach the back to the shelves. Place the top cleat flush against the top of the assembly, and fasten with screws driven through the back and into the cleat **(photo D).** Drive 1½" brads through each side panel into the ends of the top cleat and the edges of the back piece.

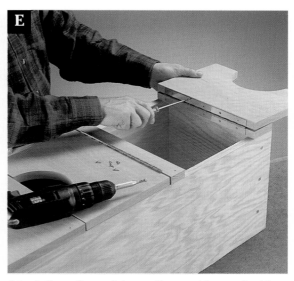

Attach the top cleat from behind with glue and screws, and set in place with two brads at each end.

Attach the rails, and then adjust and fasten the bin lids to the hinges.

MAKE THE BIN FACES AND LID. The lower bin faces are hinged for easy access. The upper bin face is permanently fixed, and access is gained through a hinged lid. Rip-cut the bin faces (F) lower rail (G), upper rail (H), lid (I) and fixed top (J) to size from 1 × 12 oak. When cutting the lid, use your circular saw to cut a 10° bevel into the back edge of the lid. On each bin face, mark a centerpoint on one long edge. Draw a 3"-rad. arc centered on each point, and cut each arc out with a jig saw. Sand the cut edges smooth.

Cut the piano hinge into two 11" sections and one 13" section, using a hacksaw. Center the 11" piano hinges on the lower and upper rails. Drill pilot holes and attach the hinges with the enclosed screws. Position the hinged rails on the bin. The lower rail should be flush with the bottom of the bin. The bottom edge of the upper rail should be flush with the middle shelf, 11¼" from the bottom of the bin. Drill pilot holes and attach the rails to the front of

the bin with glue and 1½" brads. Secure the bin faces to the hinges using the enclosed mounting hardware **(photo E).** Lay the upper bin face in position, flush with the bottom of the top shelf. Drill pilot holes and attach the upper bin face with glue and 1½" brads. Center and attach the 13" piano hinge onto the fixed top, drill pilot holes, and fasten with screws. Center the fixed top (hinge up) on top of the assembly, flush with the back edge, then drill pilot holes. Fasten with glue and 1¼" screws driven up through the top cleat into the fixed top. Attach the beveled edge of the lid to the hinge so it folds down correctly over the side panels.

MAKE THE BASE TRIM. Cut base trim sides (K) and base trim front (L) from 1 × 2 oak, and cut the quarter-round sides (M) and quarter-round front (N) to length, mitering the butting ends at 45° angles. Drill pilot holes and attach the base trim pieces with glue and 1¼" brads, and add the

quarter-round pieces above the base trim.

APPLY FINISHING TOUCHES. Fill any exposed nail holes, and finish-sand the entire project, using caution around veneered edges. Be sure to apply a non-toxic finish, such as water-based polyurethane, and let dry. Install magnetic catches in the two lower bins, and fasten stop-chains to support the lids when open **(photo F).**

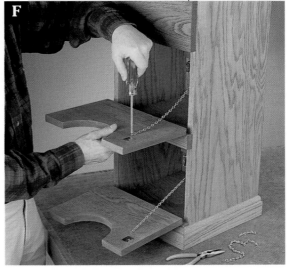

Stop-chains hold bin lids in place when open, and magnetic catches secure the lids when shut.

Bookcase

A simple, functional bookcase on which to set your picture frames, books and decorations, this project is as useful as it is attractive.

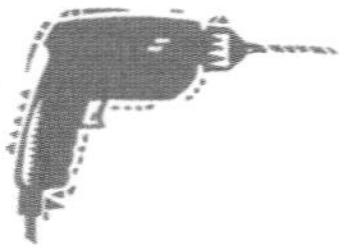

Afunctional, attractive bookcase adds just the right decorative and functional touch to a den or family room. And you don't need to shell out large amounts of cash for a high-end bookcase or settle for a cheap, throw-together particleboard unit—this sturdy bookcase looks great and will last for years.

Four roomy shelf areas let you display and store everything from framed pictures to reference manuals in the bookcase. The decorative trim on the outside of the bookcase spices up the overall appearance of the project, while cove molding along the front edges softens the corners and adds structural stability. With a few coats of enamel paint, this bookcase takes on a smooth, polished look.

Although the project is constructed mostly of plywood, the molding that fits around the top, bottom and shelves allows the bookcase to look great in almost any room of the house. This bookcase is a great-looking, useful project that you will have fun building.

CONSTRUCTION MATERIALS

Quantity	Lumber
1	¾" × 4 × 8' birch plywood
1	¼" × 4 × 8' birch plywood
2	¾ × 1⅝"× 8' panel molding
1	¾ × ¾" × 6' cove molding
2	¾ × ¾" × 8' quarter-round molding
1	¾ × 2⅝" × 6' chair-rail molding

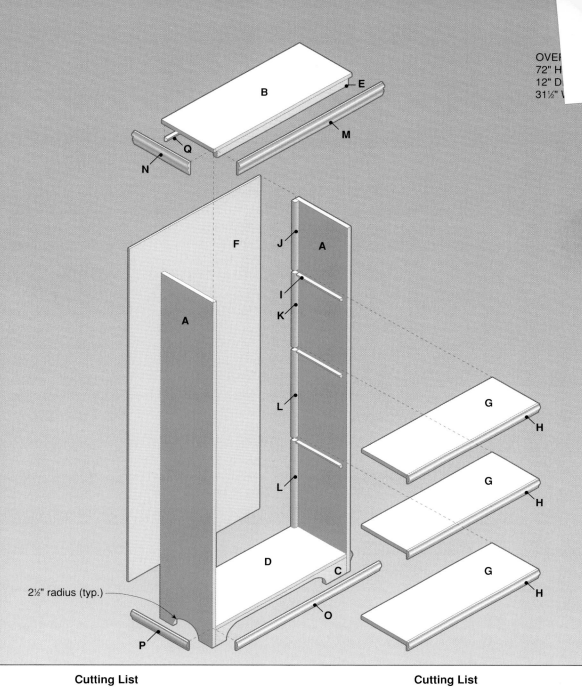

2½" radius (typ.)

Key	Part	Dimension	Pcs.	Material
A	Side	¾ × 12 × 71¼"	2	Plywood
B	Top	¾ × 11¾ × 31½"	1	Plywood
C	Front rail	¾ × 3¼ × 30"	1	Plywood
D	Bottom	¾ × 11¾ × 30"	1	Plywood
E	Top rail	¾ × 1½ × 30"	1	Plywood
F	Back	¼ × 30 × 68¾"	1	Plywood
G	Shelf	¾ × 10½ × 30"	3	Plywood
H	Shelf nosing	¾ × 1⅝ × 30"	3	Panel molding
I	Shelf cleat	¾ × ¾ × 9¾"	6	Cove molding

Cutting List

Key	Part	Dimension	Pcs.	Material
J	Back brace	¾ × ¾ × 14"	2	Quarter-round
K	Back brace	¾ × ¾ × 15"	2	Quarter-round
L	Back brace	¾ × ¾ × 18"	4	Quarter-round
M	Top facing	¾ × 2⅝ × 33"	1	Chair-rail molding
N	Top side molding	¾ × 2⅝ × 12¾"	2	Chair-rail molding
O	Bottom facing	¾ × 1⅝ × 33"	1	Panel molding
P	Bottom side molding	¾ × 1⅝ × 12¾"	2	Panel molding
Q	Back brace	¾ × ¾ × 28½"	1	Quarter-round

Materials: #6 × 2" wood screws, finish nails (4d, 6d), glue, 1¼" brads, ¾" wire nails, ¾" birch veneer edge tape (25'), finishing materials.

Note: Measurements reflect the actual thickness of dimensional lumber.

Directions: Bookcase

MAKE THE SIDES & FRONT RAIL. The bookcase sides and the front rail have arches cut into their bottom edges to create the bookcase "feet." Start by cutting the sides (A) and front rail (C) to size from ¾"-thick plywood. (We used birch plywood.) Sand the parts smooth. Clean the edges thoroughly, then cut strips of ¾" self-adhesive veneer tape slightly longer than the long

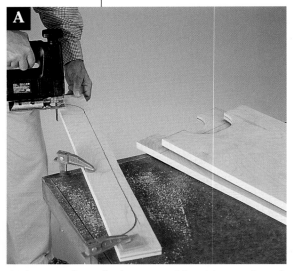

Arches cut along the bottoms of the side panels and front rail create the bookcase "feet."

edges of each side. Attach the tape by positioning it over one long edge of each side, then pressing it with a household iron set at a medium-low setting. The heat will activate the adhesive. Sand the edges and surfaces of the taped edges to smooth out any rough spots. To make the arches in the sides, designate a top and bottom to each side, and draw a cutting line across them, 2½" up from the bottom edge. Draw marks on the bottom edges of the sides, 5½" in from the front and rear edges. Set a compass to draw a 2½"-radius arc, using the marks on the bottom edges as centerpoints: set the point of the compass as close to the bottom edges of the sides as possible, and draw the arcs. Use a jig saw to cut along the lines. Repeat these steps to make the arch in the front rail, but place the point of the compass 4¾" in from each end of the front rail. Cut the front rail to shape with a jig saw **(photo A).**

BUILD THE CARCASE. The top, bottom and sides of the bookcase form the basic cabinet—

called the carcase. Begin by cutting the top (B), bottom (D) and top rail (E) to size. Sand the parts to smooth out any rough edges. Draw reference lines across the faces of the sides, 3¼" up from the bottom edges. Set the sides on edge, and position the bottom between them, just above the reference lines. Attach the bottom to the sides with glue and countersunk #6 × 2" wood screws, leaving a ¼" setback at the back edge. Set the sides upright, and position the front rail between the sides, flush with the side and bottom edges. Glue the rail ends, then clamp it to the bottom board. Drill pilot holes, and secure the front rail with 6d finish nails driven through the sides, and 1¼" brads driven through the bottom **(photo B).** Set all nail heads below the wood surface. Use glue and 6d finish nails to attach the top to the top ends of the sides, keeping the side and front edges flush. Fasten the top rail between the sides, flush with the front edges of the sides and top. Use glue and 6d finish nails to secure the top rail in place.

MAKE THE BACK. Quarter-round molding is attached on the sides and top to serve as retainer strips for the ¼"-thick plywood back. Cut the back braces (J, K, L, Q) to size from quarter-round

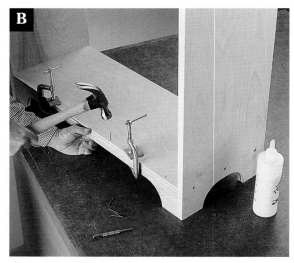

Clamp the front rail to the bottom, and fasten it with glue, finish nails and brads.

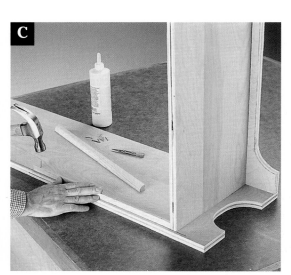

Attach the back braces to the sides, creating a ¼" recess for the back panel.

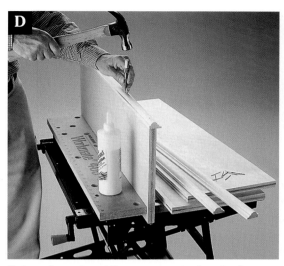

Strips of panel molding are attached to the front edges of the shelves.

Attach the shelf cleats with glue and 1¼" brads.

molding. Set the carcase on its side. Starting at the bottom, use glue and 1¼" brads to fasten the back braces to the sides and top, ¼" in from the back edges **(photo C).** Use a ¾"-thick spacer to create gaps for the shelves between the strips. Position the carcase so it rests on its front edges. Set the back in place so it rests on the back braces, and secure it with tape. Check for square by measuring diagonally from corner to corner across the back. When the measurements are the same, the carcase is square. Drive ¾" wire nails through the back and into the back braces. Do not glue the back in place.

MAKE THE SHELVES. Shelves are cut to size and inserted in the carcase between the back braces. The shelves are supported by cleats. Cut the shelves (G) and shelf nosing (H) to size. Drill pilot holes, and use glue and 4d finish nails to attach the nosing to the shelves, keeping the top edges flush **(photo D).** Set the nail heads. Cut the shelf cleats (I) to size. To help you position the shelf cleats, use a combination

square to draw reference lines square to the front edges of each side. Start the lines at the top of the lower back braces (K, L), and extend them to within 1" of the front edges of the sides. Apply glue to the shelf cleats, and position them on the reference lines. Attach the shelf cleats to the inside faces of the sides with 1¼" brads **(photo E).** Apply glue to the top edges of the shelf cleats, then slide the shelves onto the cleats. Drive 6d finish nails through the sides and into the ends of the shelves. Drive ¾" wire nails through the back panel and into the rear edges of the shelves.

APPLY FINISHING TOUCHES. Cut the top facing (M), top side molding (N), bottom facing (O) and bottom side molding (P) to size. Miter-cut both ends of the top facing and bottom facing and the front ends of the side moldings at a 45° angle so the molding pieces will fit together where they meet at the corners. Fasten the molding at the top with glue and 4d finish nails, keeping the top edges flush with the bookcase. Attach

the bottom molding, keeping the top edges flush with the bottom. To help you align the bottom side molding, draw reference lines on the sides before attaching the pieces. The reference lines should be flush with the top of the bottom facing **(photo F).** Attach the bottom side molding. Fill all holes with wood putty, and finish-sand the project. Finish as desired—we used primer and two coats of interior enamel paint.

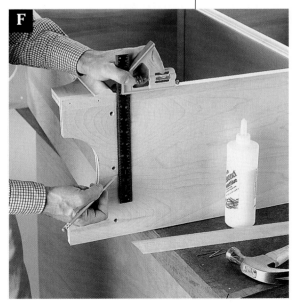

Using a combination square, draw lines on the sides, aligned with the top of the bottom facing.

Display Case

Even ordinary objects take on an air of importance in this decorative display case.

Vases, figurines, pottery, collectibles…everyone has something special that they'd like to show off to visitors. Whether your special item is a precious family heirloom or a unique project made by a child, exhibit it in fine fashion with this simple display case. The glass panels in the sides create a museum feeling, while protecting the contents of the case from dust and humidity. The sturdy top, while unprotected, also provides an effective display area for artwork or even potted plants.

This display case is built almost entirely from birch plywood and pine moldings. The viewing windows in the sides are simply cut out of the plywood side panels with a jig saw. Secure the glass with a frame made from corner molding around the outside of the opening, and rope-style glazier's compound and glazier's points in the inside of the opening. Corner and cove moldings are used to add a fanciful flair to the design. Bullet catches ensure that the top panel stays secure, but can still be removed easily when it's time for you to change the exhibit.

CONSTRUCTION MATERIALS

Quantity	Lumber
1	¾" × 4 × 4' birch plywood
2	1⅛ × 1⅛" × 8' pine corner molding
3	½ × ½" × 8' pine corner molding
1	⅝ × ⅝" × 6' cove molding

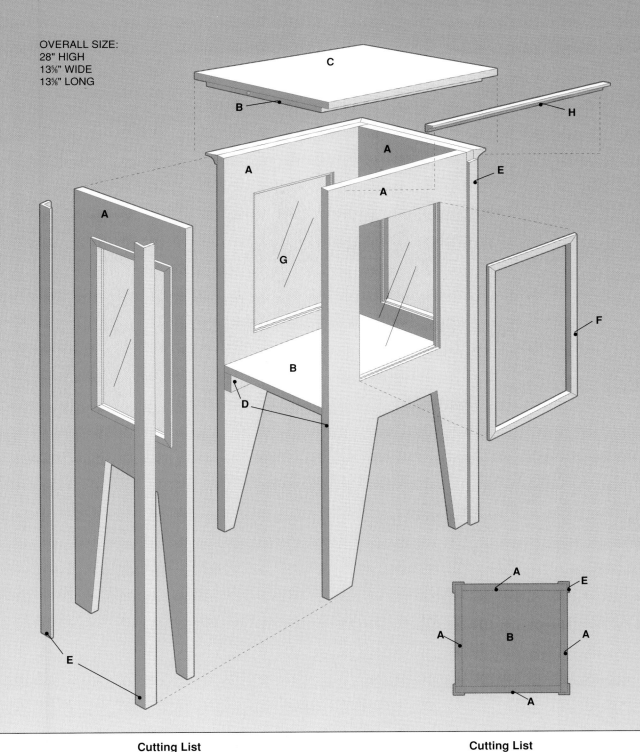

OVERALL SIZE:
28" HIGH
13⅝" WIDE
13⅝" LONG

Cutting List				
Key	**Part**	**Dimension**	**Pcs.**	**Material**
A	Side panel	¾ × 27¼ × 11¼"	4	Plywood
B	Shelf	¾ × 10½ × 10½"	2	Plywood
C	Top panel	¾ × 13⅝ × 13⅝"	1	Plywood
D	Cleat	¾ × 1½ × 10½"	4	Plywood

Cutting List				
Key	**Part**	**Dimension**	**Pcs.**	**Material**
E	Corner trim	1⅛ × 1⅛ × 26⅝"	4	Molding
F	Window trim	½ × ½ × *	16	Molding
G	Window	⅛ × 7 × 11¼"	4	Glass
H	Cove molding	⅝ × ⅝ × 13⅜"	4	Molding

Materials: Wood glue, #6 x 1¼" wood screws, 2d finish nails, glazier's points, rope-style glazier's compound.
*Cut to fit.

Note: Measurements reflect the actual size of dimensional lumber.

Make the leg and window cutouts using a jig saw.

Fasten the shelf cleats to the side panels with wood glue and screws.

Assemble the side panels with wood glue and screws to form the display case.

Directions: Display Case

MAKE THE SIDES. The side panels are each made from one piece of plywood with tapered legs and cutouts for window openings. For uniform results, follow the instructions below to make one side, then use that side as a template for laying out the other three sides. Start by cutting the side panels (A) using a circular saw and straightedge cutting guide. Mark cutting lines for the tapered legs by drawing a line across the side panels 10" from

the bottom edge. Make marks on that line 2½" from one edge, which will be the wide edge, and 1¾" from the other, narrow edge. (The legs form square corners made with butt joints—cutting one leg of each side ¾" narrower allows for square legs that are 2½" wide in each direction.) Along the bottom edge of the side panel, make marks 1½" from the wide edge and ¾" from the narrow. Draw diagonal cutting lines connecting the marks on the inside and outside edges of each leg (see *Diagram*, page 69). Cut along the cutting lines

with a jig saw to form the tapered legs, then round over the edges of legs with medium-grit (100- to 150-grit) sandpaper. The next step is to cut the window opening. Start by drawing a line across the side panel, 2" down from the top. Draw a second line across the side panel, 13¼" down from the top. Draw perpendicular lines connecting these lines, 2½" from the edge at the wide-leg side, and 1¾" from the edge at the narrow-leg side. This will result in a rectangular cutout area that is 7" wide and 11¼" high. Drill a starter hole inside a corner of the cutout area, then cut out window opening with a jig saw. Sand all edges of the side smooth, then use it as a template to mark the legs and window openings onto the other sides. Cut out the other three sides **(photo A).**

ATTACH THE SHELF CLEATS. The shelf inside the display case is supported by shelf cleats on all four sides. Cut the cleats (D) from plywood using a circular saw and straightedge cutting guide. Attach a cleat to

Mark the centers for the bullet catch receptacles on the inside surfaces of the side panels.

panel, so the top of the cleat is 1" below the window opening. One end of the cleat should be flush with the outside edge of the narrow leg. This will leave a ¾" space at the wide edge of each side panel to accept the cleat from the adjoining side. Fasten the cleats to the side panels using wood glue and #6 × 1¼" wood screws **(photo B).**

ASSEMBLE THE CASE. Apply glue to the outside edge of each narrow leg, then butt the leg against the inside face of the wide leg on the adjacent side. Drive wood screws through the wide side into the edge of the adjoining side panel. Repeat the procedure until all four side panels have been fastened **(photo C).**

INSTALL THE SHELF PANELS. Cut the two shelf panels (B) and set one aside. Sand the other shelf, then attach it to the shelf cleats with glue and wood screws—counterbore the pilot holes so the screw heads can be covered with wood putty.

MAKE & INSTALL THE TOP PANEL. Cut the top panel (C) and sand the edges smooth. Center the second shelf (B) on the underside of the top panel.

Attach it with glue and countersunk screws driven through the shelf and into the underside of the top panel. Set the top onto the top of the display case to test the fit— the shelf should fit snugly inside the frame created by the tops of the side panels. We installed bullet catches on opposite edges of the shelf to hold the top in place more securely. Drill a hole for each bullet catch in the edge of a shelf side (read the instructions on the package to find the appropriate size hole for the catches you purchase). Insert a bullet catch into each hole, then set the top back into the frame at the top of the display case. Remove the top, and check for markings from the bullet catches on the inside faces of the display case. Mark drilling points at the ends of these markings **(photo D),** then drill holes for the receptacle portions of the catches.

ATTACH THE MOLDINGS. We used pieces of corner molding and cove molding to give this display case more visual appeal. Cut strips of 1⅛" corner molding (E) the same height as the side panels, and nail them over each corner to conceal the butt joints, using 2d finish nails. Next, cut four strips of ⅝" cove molding (H) to make a frame around the top of the display case. Miter-cut the ends of the strips to make 45° miter

joints, using a power miter box or a hand miter box. Fasten the molding to the side panels with 2d finish nails. Cut the window molding (F) from corner molding. Miter-cut the corners of the frame pieces to make frames that fit inside the window openings **(photo E).**

APPLY FINISHING TOUCHES. Fill all voids and screw counterbores with wood putty, then sand all surfaces with medium (100- or 120-grit) sandpaper to smooth out rough spots. Finish-sand with fine (150- or 180-grit) sandpaper. Apply paint (we used a hard enamel paint) to all surfaces (be sure to cover the bullet catches with masking tape before painting). When the paint has dried, install the windows. Have the window glass panels (G) cut to size from ⅛"-thick glass, and insert the panels into the opening, pressed up against the edges of the corner molding frames. Press glazier's points around

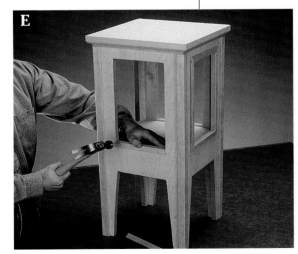

Install a frame made from corner molding around the outside edge of each window opening.

Under-bed Storage Box

*Put wasted space beneath a bed to work
with this simple roll-out storage box.*

Even a standard twin-size bed conceals 15 cubic feet or more of storage space beneath the box spring. Instead of letting that valuable space become simply a gathering spot for dust bunnies, put it to good use with this under-bed storage box. Generously proportioned and designed to roll in and out effortlessly from under your bed, it is a perfect spot to store off-season clothing, bulky sweaters, or even special mementos. And because the sliding compartment lids are made of aromatic cedar, your cherished fabric items will be safe from moths and other pests.

Construction of the under-bed storage box is very simple. It is basically a pine frame with a center divider and cleats for the lids and the bottom panels. We mounted bed-box rollers at all four corners so the box can slide in and out easily. Bed-box rollers are specialty hardware

items that can be purchased at most hardware stores or woodworker's stores. Because they are hard plastic, they will not damage or discolor carpeting.

The pine, plywood and cedar used in the under-bed storage box make it suitable for just about any type of finish. Because it spends most of its time under the bed, you may prefer not to spend a lot of time and effort creating a beautiful finish. But you should at least seal the pine and plywood with a clear topcoat for protection. We painted the box as well to give it a little more appeal. Do not apply a finish to the aromatic cedar if you want it to retain its fragrance.

CONSTRUCTION MATERIALS

Quantity	Lumber
3	1 × 2" × 8' pine
2	1 × 3" × 8' pine
2	1 × 6" × 8' pine
1	⅜" × 4 × 8' BC plywood
1	¼" × 4 × 8' aromatic cedar

OVERALL SIZE:
5½" HIGH
30" WIDE
60" LONG

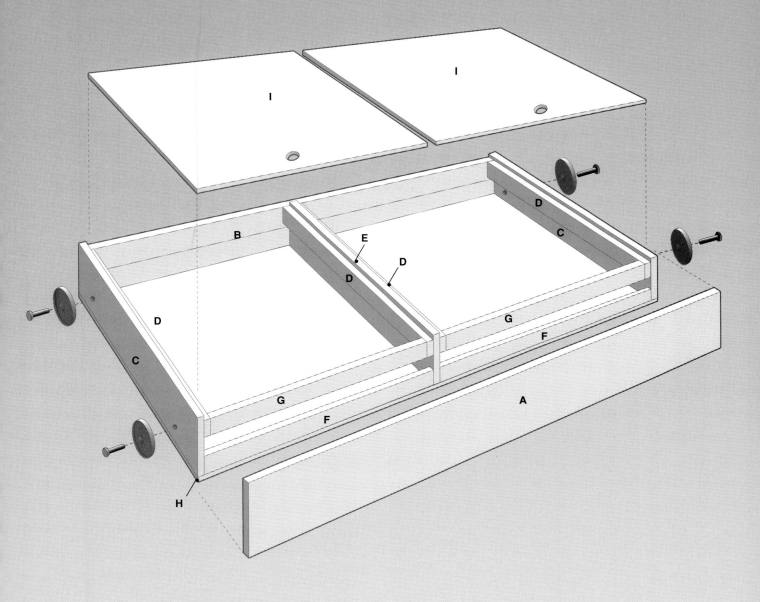

		Cutting List						Cutting List		
Key	Part	Dimension	Pcs.	Material		Key	Part	Dimension	Pcs.	Material
A	Box front	¾ × 5½ × 60"	1	Pine		F	Bottom cleat	¾ × 1½ × 27¾"	2	Pine
B	Box back	¾ × 2½ × 56½"	2	Pine		G	Top cleat	¾ × 1½ × 26¼"	2	Pine
C	Box side	¾ × 5½ × 29¼"	2	Pine		H	Bottom panel	⅜ × 29¼ × 58"	1	Plywood
D	Lid support	¾ × 1½ × 28½"	4	Pine		I	Sliding lid	¼ × 27¾ × 29¼"	2	Aromatic cedar
E	Divider	¾ × 5½ × 28½"	1	Pine						

Materials: Bed-box rollers w/mounting bolts, #6 × 1¼" and #6 × 2" wood screws, wood glue.

Note: Measurements reflect the actual size of dimensional lumber.

Directions:
Under-bed Storage Box

MAKE THE FRAME. The frame for the under-bed storage box is a basic box made with butt joints. The front board on the box overhangs the sides by 1" to conceal the front bed-box rollers that are mounted to the sides. Cut the box front (A) and box sides (C) to size from 1 × 6 pine, and cut the box back (B) parts from 1 × 3 pine (when laid edge to edge, two 1 × 3s are ½" shorter than one 1 × 6, which will create a recess for mounting the bottom panel). Sand all parts smooth. Draw a reference line on the inside face of the box front, 1" in from each side. Set the box front on a spacer made from ½" plywood. Align the box sides at the inside edges of the reference lines (check to make sure the top of the box front is ⁵⁄₁₆" higher than the tops of the side), and attach them to the front with glue and #6 × 2" wood screws—counterbore the screws so the heads can be covered with wood putty. Attach one of the box back 1 × 3s between the sides, flush with the bottom edges, using glue and screws. Attach the other 1 × 3 between the sides, making sure the edges of the two back parts are butted together

Fasten the back between the sides using wood glue and counterbored screws. Use wood spacer blocks to keep bottom edges flush.

Clamp the lid supports in position flush with the tops of the box front and back, then fasten them with wood glue and screws.

tightly, and there is a ½" gap between the top of the back and the sides **(photo A)**.

INSTALL THE FRAME DIVIDER & CLEATS. Mark centerpoints on the inside faces of the box front and box backs: the front centerpoint is 30" from the ends; the back centerpoint is 28¼" from the ends (measure from the ends of the back, not the outside faces of the box). Cut the divider (E), then position it between the front and back of the box, with the end of the divider centered on the centerpoints. The top of the divider should be

⁵⁄₁₆" above the tops of the front and back. Attach the divider with glue and screws driven through the front and back and into the ends of the divider. Cut the lid supports (D), top cleats (G), and bottom cleats (F). Attach the lid supports to the sides of the divider, flush with the tops of the front and back. Use glue and #6 × 1¼" wood screws **(photo B).** Attach the bottom cleats to the inside face of the box front, flush with the bottom edges of the sides. Position the top cleats between the lid supports, against the inside face of

If the top and bottom cleats are too long, mark them against the opening for trimming.

Cut the bottom panel to size, then fasten it to the bottom edges of the box frame and divider.

Mount bed-box rollers on the outside faces of the sides so the rollers extend ½" below the box bottom.

the box front. If the cleats are too long, mark them for trimming to length **(photo C).** Attach the top cleats to the inside face of the box front, flush with the tops of the lid supports.

ATTACH THE BOTTOM PANEL. Cut the bottom panel (H) to size from ⅜" plywood. Turn the frame assembly upside down and apply glue to the bottom edges of the frame components. Fasten the bottom panel to the frame assembly by driving screws through the bottom into the edges of the frame and the divider **(photo D).**

INSTALL THE SLIDING LIDS. Cut the sliding lids (I) to size from ¼"-thick aromatic cedar pressboard. Mark centerpoints (13⅞" from the sides) 2" in from the front edge of each lid. Drill 1"-dia. holes through the centerpoints to create finger grips for sliding the lids back and forth. Sand all edges of the lids, as well as the finger-grip cutouts, to prevent splinters when handling the lids. The lids are designed to simply rest on the lid supports between the divider and the sides of the frame. Because they are not

attached permanently, they can be lifted off for easy access, in addition to sliding back and forth on the lid supports. If you are using the under-bed storage box in a spot where it may be kicked or jostled frequently, you can hold the lids in place more securely by driving finish nails into the inside faces of the sides and dividers, just above the lid.

APPLY THE FINISHING TOUCHES. Fill all counterbored screw holes with wood putty, then sand the entire unit with fine (120- to 150-grit) sandpaper. Install the bed-box rollers on the outside faces of the sides, 3" in from the front and the back. The rollers should extend ½" below the bottom edges of the sides **(photo E).** Remove the rollers and axles for finishing. We painted the storage box, then topcoated it with polyurethane (except for the cedar lids, which were left unfinished). Reinstall the rollers and mount chest handles or straps (optional) on the front to make the box easier to slide in and out from under the bed.

Nightstand

A back rail adds style to our nightstand and keeps you from knocking bedside items to the floor. Put our nightstand at your bedside for a classic touch of bedroom beauty.

Our nightstand is a classic piece of furniture that will never go out of fashion. Ours is a simple nightstand with a solid, traditional look. The arched back rail and base pieces add some style and grace to the project, while the handy drawer gives you a great place to store some bedside items.

Assembling this little beauty is an easy process. You first build the box frame. The box frame is the central section of the nightstand, and decorative items are built around it. The box frame is made by attaching the sides, back and shelves. It is then topped off with a decorative back rail and wings. These pieces do more than dress up the nightstand—they reduce the risk of knocking over that insistent alarm clock when you lurch over to shut it off in the morning.

Once the top sections are complete, you then make the arched base and attach the two sections. The drawer comes next, and we avoided expen-

sive metal track glides. Instead, we used friction reducing plastic bumpers and tack-on glides for easy installation and convenience.

Our nightstand is built from edge-glued "ponderosa" pine panels that you can purchase at most building centers. These panels come in varying widths, so be aware that the dimensions shown here are for ¾"-thick boards.

CONSTRUCTION MATERIALS

Quantity	Lumber
2	1 × 16" × 8' edge-glued pine
1	1 × 4" × 4' pine

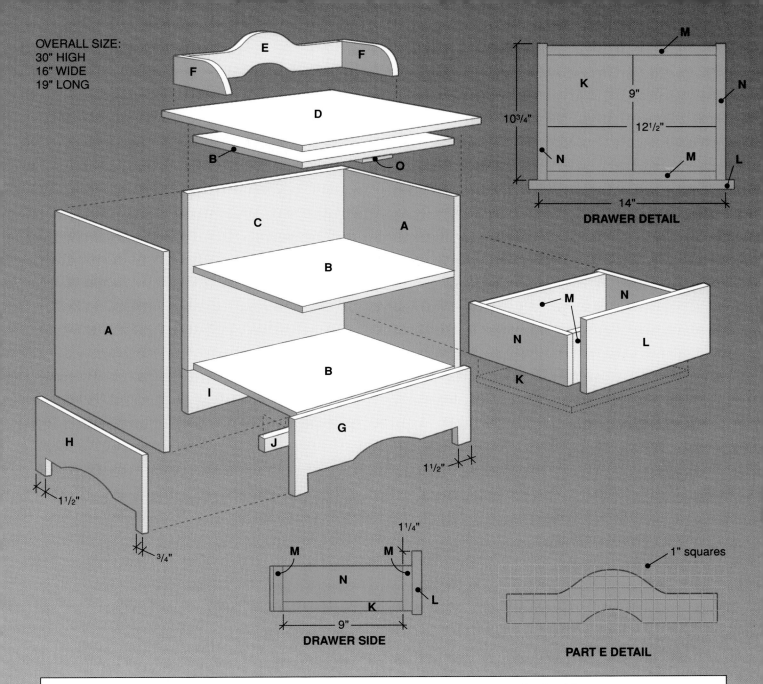

OVERALL SIZE:
30" HIGH
16" WIDE
19" LONG

E F

F

D

B

O

C A

B

B

A

I

G

H J

1½"

1½"

¾"

DRAWER DETAIL

M

K 9" N

10¾" 12½"

N M L

14"

M N

N L

K

DRAWER SIDE

1¼"

M M

N

L

K

9"

PART E DETAIL

1" squares

Cutting List

Key	Part	Dimension	Pcs.	Material
A	Side	¾ × 13¼ × 17"	2	Pine
B	Shelf	¾ × 13¼ × 14½"	3	Pine
C	Back	¾ × 16 × 17"	1	Pine
D	Top	¾ × 16 × 19"	1	Pine
E	Back rail	¾ × 4½ × 17½"	1	Pine
F	Wing	¾ × 2½ × 5½"	2	Pine
G	Base front	¾ × 8 × 17½"	1	Pine
H	Base side	¾ × 8 × 14"	2	Pine

Cutting List

Key	Part	Dimension	Pcs.	Material
I	Base back	¾ × 4 × 16"	1	Pine
J	Base cleat	¾ × 2 × 16"	1	Pine
K	Drawer bottom	¾ × 9 × 12½"	1	Pine
L	Drawer front	¾ × 5 × 15¾"	1	Pine
M	Drawer end	¾ × 3½ × 12½"	2	Pine
N	Drawer side	¾ × 3½ × 10¾"	2	Pine
O	Stop cleat	¾ × 1½ × 3"	1	Pine

Materials: Glue, wood screws (1¼, 1½, 2"), ¾"-dia. wooden knobs, 4d finish nails, plastic drawer stop, tack-on drawer glides, stem bumpers, finishing materials.

Note: Measurements reflect the actual size of dimensional lumber.

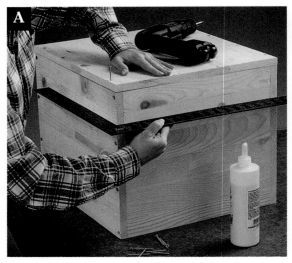
Attach the back to one side, then check for square.

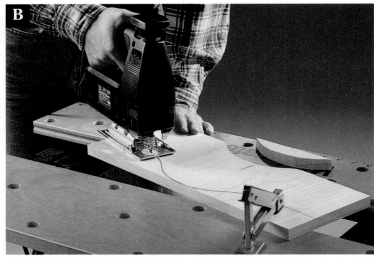
Trace the pattern, then cut the back rail to shape with a jig saw.

Directions: Nightstand

ATTACH THE SHELVES & SIDES. Start by cutting the sides (A) and shelves (B) to size. Sand the pieces to finished smoothness. Use glue and #6 × 2" countersunk wood screws to attach the top and bottom shelves flush with the top and bottom side edges. You will attach the middle shelf later in the assembly process. Make sure the screws are centered and the front and back shelf edges are flush with the side edges.

ATTACH THE BACK. Start by cutting the back to size. Sand the back to finished smoothness, then attach it to one side with glue and countersunk wood screws **(photo A).** Check the outside of the frame to be sure the sides are square with the shelves. If they are not square, you must apply pressure to one side to draw the pieces square. This can be done by hand or by attaching a bar clamp diagonally from one side to the other. When the

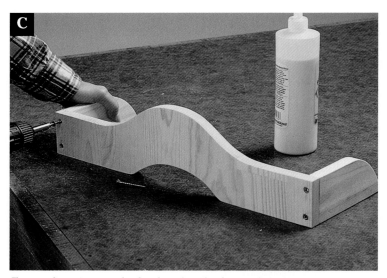
Fasten the wings to the back rail with glue and deck screws.

pieces are square, clamp them and continue to attach the back to the sides and shelves.

MAKE & ATTACH THE TOP ASSEMBLY. The top assembly consists of four pieces: the top (D), back rail (E) and wings (F). Start by cutting them to size. Transfer the grid on page 77 to a piece of stiff cardboard, making a cutting template for the back rail (see *Tip*, page 79). Trace the shape onto the back rail, and use a jig saw to cut it to finished shape **(photo B).**

Position the template you made for the back rail along the inside faces of the wing. Trace along the template arc to make a partial arc at the wing ends. Cut a smooth curve on the end of each wing. Make sure the curves on the wings are identical. Sand all the pieces to finished smoothness. Drill pilot holes in the back rail to attach the wings. The pilot holes should be positioned ⅜"

Draw the guidelines on the top, then drill the pilot holes and attach the back rail and wings.

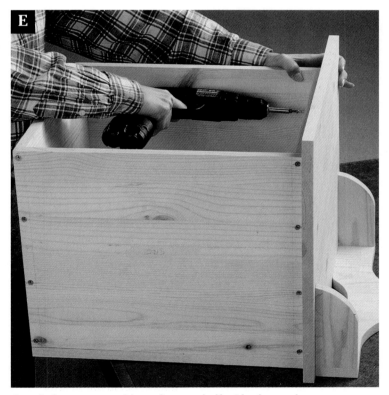

Attach the top assembly to the top shelf with glue and screws.

TIP

When transferring a grid diagram, consider these options. You can enlarge the grid diagram on a copier, and trace it onto a piece of cardboard to form a tracing template. Or, you can grid your stock with 1" squares and draw the pattern directly onto the workpiece. Both options are easy and convenient.

Finally, attach the back rail and wings to the top with wood screws and glue **(photo D).** Center the top assembly over the top shelf, with the back edges flush. Attach the top assembly by driving countersunk #6 × 1¼" wood screws through the top shelf into the top assembly **(photo E).**

ATTACH THE MIDDLE SHELF. Start by measuring and marking guidelines on the inside edges of the sides for the remaining shelf. Position the top of the middle shelf 5½" down from the tops of the sides. Fasten the shelf between the sides with screws and glue. This shelf will support the drawer, so make sure it is square to the sides. With the completion of this step, the nightstand box frame is complete.

MAKE THE BASE. Start by cutting the base front (G), base sides (H), base back (I) and base cleat (J) to size. Position the template made for the back rail onto the base front and base sides so that the top of the arc is 3" from the top of each piece. Center the template on the base front, but position it ¾" from the front edges on the sides (see *Diagram*, page 77).

from the outside edges. Fasten the wings to the back rail with glue and countersunk #6 × 1½" wood screws **(photo C).** Drill pilot holes along the back edge to attach the back rail. Position the back rail and wings onto the top with the back rail flush with the top's back edge. Draw a 5½"-long line marking the outside edges of the wings. Make sure the distance between the wings' outside edges and the top edge is ¾". Drill pilot holes ⅜" inside each line on the top to attach each wing. Sand the top to finished smoothness.

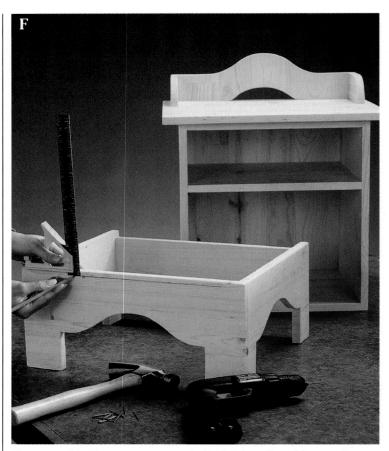

Use a combination square to mark the finish nail position on the base front.

Trace the arcs, and cut the designs from the pieces with a jig saw. Sand the parts smooth. Use glue and 4d finish nails to fasten the base front to the base sides. Fasten the base back between the base sides so that its top edge is ½" below the top edges of the base sides. Finally, attach the base cleat to the inside of the base front with #6 × 1¼" wood screws. Leave a ½" space between the top edge of the cleat and the top edge of the base. Once you have attached the cleat, the base is complete.

ATTACH THE FRAME & BASE. Start by marking a guideline ¼" below the top edge of the base front and base sides **(photo F).** Use a combination square to make it easy to scribe an accurate guideline. Carefully position the nightstand box frame into the base so that it rests on the base back and base cleat. Fasten the box frame to the base by driving finish nails along the guidelines through the base front and base sides, and into the edges of the bottom shelf.

BUILD THE DRAWER. Cut the drawer bottom (K), drawer front (L), drawer ends (M), and drawer sides (N). Measure and mark a line along the inside face of each drawer side, ¼" from the back edge, to mark the position of the rear drawer end. Drill pilot holes along the drawer ends, ⅜" above the bottom edges, and attach the drawer ends to the drawer bottom with counterbored wood screws and glue. Align the drawer sides so their front edges are flush with the front faces of the ends. Drill pilot holes through the sides, and fasten the sides to the bottom and ends with #6 × 1½" wood screws and glue **(photo G).** Sand the drawer and drawer front to smooth the edges and prepare the surfaces for finish application.

ATTACH THE DRAWER FRONT. To align the drawer front with the drawer, you must measure and mark three lines. Mark a line along the inside face of the drawer front ¼" above the bottom edge. Mark another line down the center of the drawer front. Finally, mark a centerline on the top edge of the front drawer end. Fasten the drawer end to the drawer front so the bottom of the front is on the ¼" line, and the center marks are in line. Use countersunk #6 × 1¼" wood screws driven through the drawer end into the drawer front **(photo H).**

INSTALL THE STOP CLEAT. When used in conjunction with a store-bought drawer stop, the stop cleat will prevent the drawer from falling out of the nightstand if you pull too hard. Start by cutting the stop cleat

(O) to size. Center the stop cleat beneath the top shelf, and attach it with glue and screws. The front edge of the stop cleat should be ¾" behind the front of the top shelf.

INSTALL THE HARDWARE. You have a number of options in making the drawer a functioning element of the nightstand. For instance, you can use metal glides that attach permanently to the drawer and frame. We used inexpensive plastic glides and stem bumpers. The Teflon®-coated glides have metal points and are installed like thumbtacks for easy application. Glue and insert the stem bumpers into drilled holes on the drawer bottom. You can buy these glides and bumpers at any building center. Always follow manufacturer's directions when installing the hardware, no matter what type you use. Start by fastening the wooden knobs to the drawer front. Be sure to space the wooden knobs evenly. Attach the glides. Finally, drill a ³⁄₁₆"-dia. hole on the rear drawer end for the drawer stop. A drawer stop is a small piece of plastic with a long stem that contacts the stop cleat when the drawer is opened, preventing it from sliding all the way out. Make the hole ½" below the drawer end's top edge. Glue and insert the drawer stop. Insert the drawer. With the drawer open slightly, reach in and turn the drawer stop until it is in position to touch the stop cleat.

APPLY FINISHING TOUCHES. Fill all the screw holes, and sand all the surfaces until they are completely smooth. Paint the nightstand inside and out, including the drawer, and apply a polyurethane topcoat to protect the painted finish.

TIP

Edge-glued pine paneling, sometimes known as "ponderosa paneling," is a fairly new product. Generally sold in 10-20" widths at building centers, these panels are often encased in plastic wrap and displayed with the shelving products.

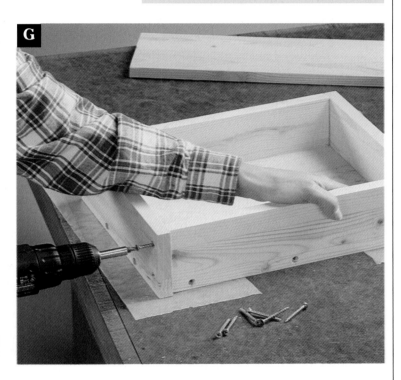

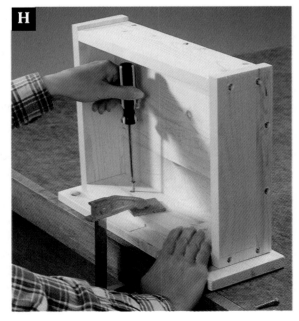

(above) Fasten the drawer sides to the drawer ends and drawer bottom with glue and wood screws.

(left) Align the drawer front and attach the pieces by driving wood screws through the drawer end.

Drawing Board

*Give your kids a good alternative to wall graffiti
with this erasable drawing board.*

CONSTRUCTION MATERIALS

Quantity	Lumber
6	1 × 2" × 8' pine
3	1 × 4" × 8' pine
1	1 × 6" × 4' pine
1	½" × 4 × 4' AB plywood
1	½ × 1¼" × 4' stop molding
1	¼" × 2 × 4' white melamine
1	½ × 12 × 36" cork sheet/tile

It's an unexplained fact of nature that kids love to draw on walls. With this combination drawing board and bulletin board, you can confine your childrens' artistic inclinations to a suitable spot—and have a place to display drawings and artwork to boot.

The slick melamine surface on this drawing board erases easily and cleanly when common dry-erase markers are used. Nontoxic and available in an array of colors, dry-erase markers are sold at any office or school supply store. The cork used to make the bulletin board can be purchased as a sheet or in tile form from art or craft supply stores, or from just about any building center.

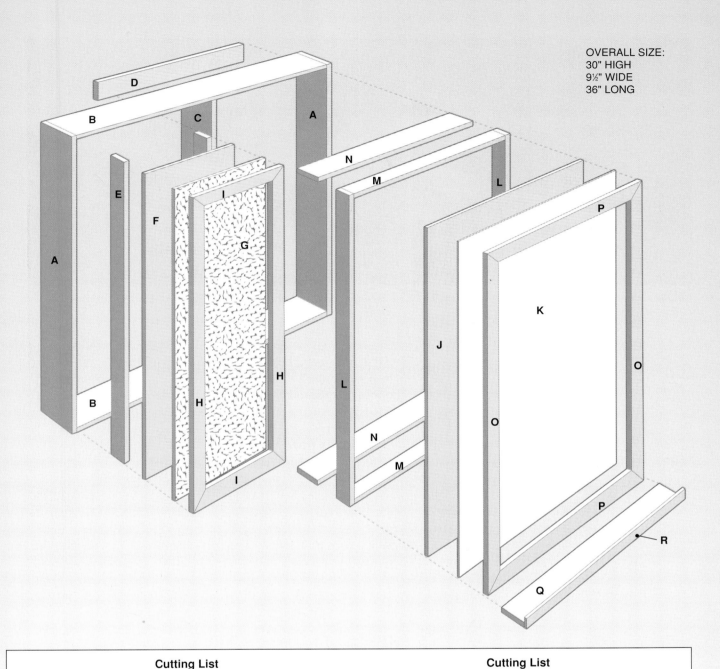

OVERALL SIZE:
30" HIGH
9½" WIDE
36" LONG

Key	Part	Dimension	Pcs.	Material
Cutting List				
A	Frame side	¾ × 3½ × 30"	2	Pine
B	Frame end	¾ × 3½ × 34½"	2	Pine
C	Stringer	¾ × 3½ × 28½"	1	Pine
D	Ledger	¾ × 3½ × 23¼"	1	Pine
E	Backer cleat	¾ × 1½ × 28½"	2	Pine
F	Cork backer	½ × 10½ × 28½"	1	Plywood
G	Cork board	½ × 10½ × 28½"	1	Cork tile/strip
H	Cork retainer side	¾ × 1½ × 30"	2	Pine
I	Cork retainer end	¾ × 1½ × 12"	2	Pine

Key	Part	Dimension	Pcs.	Material
Cutting List				
J	Board backer	½ × 22½ × 28½"	1	Pine
K	Marking board	¼ × 22½ × 28½"	1	Melamine
L	Board frame side	¾ × 1½ × 30"	2	Pine
M	Board frame end	¾ × 1½ × 22½"	2	Pine
N	Board cleat	¾ × 3½ × 22½"	2	Pine
O	Board retainer side	¾ × 1½ × 30"	2	Pine
P	Board retainer end	¾ × 1½ × 24"	2	Pine
Q	Marker tray	¾ × 5½ × 24"	1	Pine
R	Tray lip	½ × 1¼ × 24"	1	Pine

Materials: Wood glue, #6 × 1½" and #8 × 3" wood screws, finish nails (4d, 6d), wood plugs, pine-tinted wood putty, and finishing materials.

Note: Measurements reflect the actual size of dimensional lumber.

Clamp the main frame sides and ends together, and drill counterbored pilot holes at the joints.

Position the ledger between the stringer and right frame side and secure in place with wood glue and screws.

Directions:
Drawing Board

MAKE THE MAIN FRAME. The main frame for this drawing board houses the smaller frames that wrap the marker board and the bulletin board. Cut the frame sides (A) and frame ends (B) to length from 1 × 4 pine. Position the frame ends between the frame sides, to create a box frame. Use bar or pipe clamps to hold the frame together while you drill pilot holes through the sides and into the frame ends. Counterbore the pilot holes deeply enough to accept ⅜"-dia. wood plugs **(photo A).** Unclamp the frame, then apply wood glue to the ends of the frame ends and the mating surfaces of the frame sides. Fasten the frame components together with #6 × 1½" wood screws. Cut the stringer (C) and ledger (D) to length from 1 × 4 pine. Attach the stringer between the frame ends, so it is 12" from the left side of the frame. Use glue and counterbored screws. Next, position the ledger between the stringer and the right frame

side, flush with the back edge of the stringer and butted up to the inside surface of the top frame end **(photo B).** The ledger is used as an anchoring surface for mounting the drawing board to a wall. Secure the ledger with glue and screws driven through the frame side and the stringer. On the bulletin board side of the main frame (the left side), draw reference lines 1" in from the front edges of the left frame side and the stringer. The reference lines are used as guides for installing the backer cleats for the bulletin board. The 1" recess allows room for the backer and the cork panel to fit

TIP

An alternative to using melamine for a dry-erase writing board is to use a chalkboard panel. Chalkboard traditionally was made from solid slate. But these days, it is more commonly sold as a specially coated particleboard available in sheet form in thicknesses from ¼" to ½".

flush with the front edges of the frame opening. Cut the backer cleats (E) to length, then attach the cleats to the frame, just inside the reference lines, with glue and screws.

MAKE THE BULLETIN BOARD. The bulletin board is simply a plywood backer board and a ½"-thick cork panel, held in place by a mitered frame made from 1 × 2" pine. Build the bulletin board by cutting the cork backer (F) to size from ½"-thick plywood and fastening it to the backer cleats on the frame with glue and screws. Next, cut the cork surface (G). You can use either strips of ¼"- to ½"- thick cork, or cork tiles. Position the cork material onto the backer board **(photo C)**—use panel adhesive to hold it in place if necessary. Next, make the retainer-strip frame that holds the cork surface and the backer board in place. Cut the cork retainer sides (H) and ends (I) to length from 1 × 2, mitering the corners at 45° to create a frame with square corners. Fasten the retainer frame pieces to the main frame side using glue and 6d finish nails. Be sure to drill

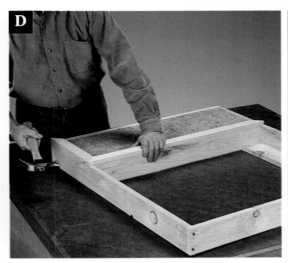

Cut the cork tiles or strips to size, and position them on top of the cork backer board.

Drive a 6d finish nail through each miter joint to lock it together—be sure to drill pilot holes.

pilot holes for the finish nails to prevent splitting the wood. After the retainer frame is built and attached to the main frame, drive one 6d finish nail through a pilot hole in each joint to lock-nail the mitered corners together **(photo D)**.

MAKE THE MARKER BOARD. The marker board is similar in construction to the bulletin board, except that the marker board has a full frame both behind and in front of the primary surface. Start the marker board construction by cutting the board frame sides (L) and board frame ends (M) to length from 1 × 2 pine. Fasten the ends between the sides with glue and screws. Be sure to drill counterbored pilot holes for all screws. Draw a reference line ¾" in from the front edges of each board frame end. Cut the board cleats (N) to length and fasten them at the back sides of the reference lines with glue and screws. Cut the board backer (J) to size from ½"-thick plywood and fasten it to the board cleats with glue and screws. Cut the marking board (K) to size from ¼"-thick white

melamine and place it against the board backer. Cut the board retainer sides (O) and ends (P) to size to make a retainer frame for the marking board, following the same steps as for the cork retainer frame. Fasten the retaining frame to the board frame with glue and 6d nails.

MAKE & ATTACH THE MARKER TRAY. The marker tray is designed to hold dry-erase markers and erasers for quick and easy access. It has a lip in front to keep utensils and supplies from falling onto the floor. Cut the marker tray (Q) to length from 1 × 6 pine and cut the tray lip (R) to length from ½"-thick × 1¼"-wide stop molding. Attach the tray lip to the marker tray with glue and 4d finish nails. Fasten the marker shelf to the underside of the main frame, flush at the ends and back edge of the frame, using glue and countersunk #6 × 1½" screws **(photo E)**.

APPLY FINISHING TOUCHES. Finish-sand the entire project and fill all counterbore holes with pine wood plugs, and use pine-tinted wood putty as

needed to fill any other holes or scratches. Apply your finish of choice. We used plain orange shellac (which both colors and protects the wood). When finished, hang the drawing board on your wall by driving #8 × 3" screws through the ledger and into wall stud locations. Check the drawing board with a level before driving the screws. Insert the marker board into the opening in the main frame, and drive screws through the main frame sides and into the marker board sides, fastening the drawing board together.

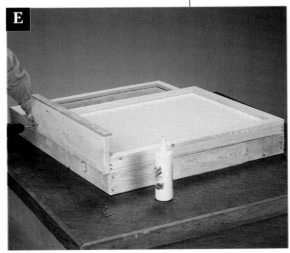

Fasten the marker tray to the underside of the main frame, using glue and screws.

Toy Drop-box

Designed to look like a mailbox and work like a toy chest, this fun project will fascinate your kids and inspire them to keep their favorite toys where they belong.

The design for this toy chest was based on the idea that the more interesting a child finds a piece of furniture, the more likely he or she is to use it. In addition to the striking appearance based on a postal drop-box, this toy chest has two loading points, one at the top and one at the front, to make it more interactive for your child. Soft toys can be dropped into the top opening, but more fragile playthings can be loaded carefully through the front opening. Self-closing hinges on the front ensure that the door stays closed, without the hazards created by latches that cannot be operated from inside. Rounded corners on the hinged top lid are very forgiving if they get bumped by a child.

Your kids will love this toy drop-box because it is fun and interactive. You will love it because it is easy and inexpensive to make. The entire project is constructed from two sheets of plywood—we used birch plywood because it has smooth, splinter-free surfaces that are excellent for painting. The rounded tops of the toy drop-box sides are easy to mark and cut, and even the rail structure that supports the hinged lid is very easy to make and install.

We painted our toy drop-box blue to stay with the postal box theme. But the broad flat surfaces present many options if you decide to be more creative: sponge painting or applying colorful decals are just two of the possibilities.

CONSTRUCTION MATERIALS

Quantity	Lumber
1	¾" × 4 × 8' birch plywood
1	¾" × 4 × 4' birch plywood

OVERALL SIZE:
48" HIGH
24" WIDE
25½" LONG

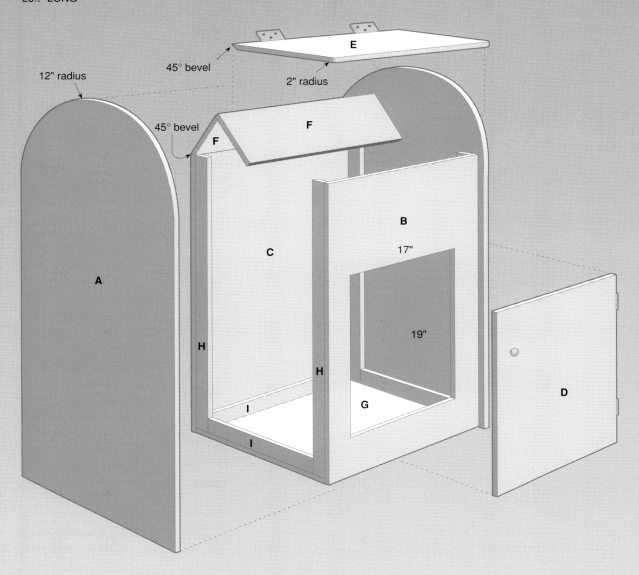

12" radius

45° bevel

2" radius

45° bevel

E

F

F

F

A

C

B

17"

19"

H

H

H

I

G

D

I

Cutting List				
Key	**Part**	**Dimension**	**Pcs.**	**Material**
A	Side panel	¾ × 24 × 48"	2	Plywood
B	Front panel	¾ × 24 × 37½"	1	Plywood
C	Back panel	¾ × 24 × 37½"	1	Plywood
D	Door	¾ × 18 × 20"	1	Plywood
E	Lid	¾ × 14 × 23¾"	1	Plywood

Cutting List				
Key	**Part**	**Dimension**	**Pcs.**	**Material**
F	Top rail	¾ × 7½ × 24"	2	Plywood
G	Bottom panel	¾ × 1½ × 17½"	1	Plywood
H	Side cleat	¾ × 1 × 36¾"	4	Plywood
I	Bottom cleat	¾ × 1 × 19½"	2	Plywood

Materials: Wood glue, #6 × 1¼" wood screws, wood filler, hinges, finishing materials, nail-on glide feet.

Note: Measurements reflect the actual size of dimensional lumber.

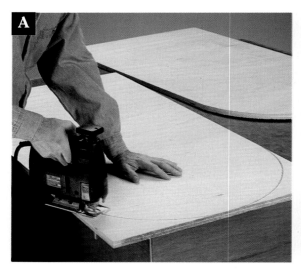

Draw semicircular cutting lines at the tops of the side panels, then cut with a jig saw.

Lay out the side and bottom cleat positions on the side panels, then attach the cleats with wood glue and screws.

Draw the rectangular cutout for the front door opening on the front panel, then drill a starter hole and make the cutout with a jig saw.

Directions: Toy Drop-Box

BUILD THE SIDE PANELS. The side panels have rounded tops that are cut with a jig saw, and the inside surfaces are cleated to create screwing surfaces for the other parts of the basic box construction. Cut the side panels (A). On one of the panels, measure down 12" from the top edge and 12" in from the side, then mark a point. Drive a finish nail at this point, then tie a string to the nail. Tie a pencil to the string, 12" out from the nail, pull the string taut, and draw a sweeping semicircle from side to side to make the cutting line for the top roundover. Cut along the line with a jig saw, then sand the cut smooth. Use this side panel as a template to mark a matching cutting line on the other side panel, then cut and sand the second side panel **(photo A).** To ensure that the sides are completely uniform, clamp them together face to face so the tops are as closely aligned as possible. Sand both roundovers at the same time with a power sander

until they are shaped exactly alike. Trim all edges with a router and a ¼" roundover bit, or use a power sander to smooth out the sharp edges. Cut the side cleats (H) and bottom cleats (I). On the inside surfaces of the side panels, lay out the locations for the cleats. The vertical side cleats should be placed 1¼" in from the front and back edges of the side panels. This will allow for a ½" setback once the front and back panels are installed. The bottom cleats should be ¾" up from the bottoms of the side panels to allow room for the bottom panel. Attach the cleats with glue and #6 × 1¼" wood screws **(photo B).**

MAKE THE FRONT, BACK & BOTTOM PANELS. Cut the front panel (B), back panel (C) and bottom panel (G) to size from birch plywood. On the front panel, lay out a 17 × 19" door opening, 5" up from the bottom and 3½" in from each side. Drill a ⅜"-dia. starter hole on the inside of each corner, then cut the opening with a jig saw **(photo C).** Sand all the edges smooth.

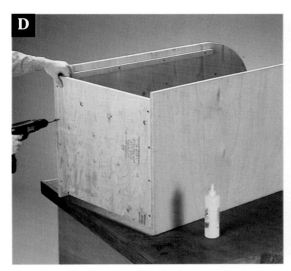

Fasten the bottom panel to the bottom cleats on the side panels.

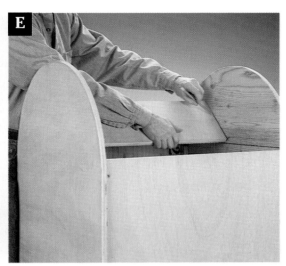

Outline the top rail assembly for reference, then fasten it with glue and screws.

ASSEMBLE THE BOX. To assemble the box components (the front, sides, back and bottom panels), simply arrange the parts together so the front and back match up with the cleats on the inside surfaces of the side frame. Then, fasten the parts together with glue and wood screws—be sure to counterbore the screw pilot holes slightly so they can be filled with wood putty to cover the screw heads. Cut the bottom panel (G) and fasten it to the undersides of the bottom cleats—it should fit snugly inside the front, sides, and back **(photo D).**

MAKE & INSTALL THE TOP RAILS. The top rails are butted together at the top of the toy drop-box, where they fit against the sides in an inverted "V" position. Their function is largely decorative, but the front rail does support the hinges for the lid. Cut the top rails (F) to size: on one of the rails (to be used in the back position), cut a 45° bevel at the back edge. The bevel fits against the top edge of the back panel. Butt the two rails together to form a V-shape,

with the beveled edge away from the joint. Join the rails with glue and screws. Now, draw reference lines across the inside faces of the side panels, connecting the top edges of the front and back panels. Position the rail assembly so the beveled edge is flat against the top edge of the back panel, and the other free end is flush against the reference lines on the side panels **(photo E).** Drill counterbored pilot holes through the centers of the outlines, then attach the rail assembly with glue and screws.

ATTACH THE LID & DOOR. Cut the lid (E) and the door (D) to size from plywood, cutting a 45° bevel on the rear edge of the lid so it opens and closes without contacting the top rails. Use a compass to mark a 2"-radius roundover at the outside corners of the lid. Smooth out sharp edges on the lid and door using a router with a ¼" roundover bit, or a power sander. Fasten butt hinges to the lid, 2" in from each end, then mount the lid to the front edge of the top rail assembly. Mount the front door to the

front panel with self-closing hinges, allowing for a ½" overlap on all sides of the door opening **(photo F).**

APPLY FINISHING TOUCHES. Fill all counterbores and exposed plywood edges with wood putty. Sand smooth and apply your finish of choice (we used blue enamel paint). Attach nail-on glide feet to the bottoms of the side panels, and attach a door pull to the front door.

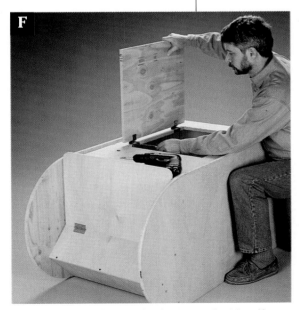

Attach the front door to the front panel with self-closing hinges, positioning the door with a ½" overhang on all sides.

Exterior Light Post

Your yard, deck, or patio will sparkle in the evening with this rustic outdoor light post.

CONSTRUCTION MATERIALS

Quantity	Lumber
2	1 × 8" × 6' cedar
1	1 × 10" × 2' cedar
1	1⁄16" × 2 × 2' acrylic

Lighting is an important but often overlooked element in landscape design. Our sturdy light post brings increased safety, security and attractiveness to any outdoor setting.

Made of durable, easy-to-machine cedar boards, this light post can be positioned to highlight plantings, illuminate walkways or to let you check on outdoor noises at the flip of a switch.

The top of our light post is held firmly in place with invisible roller catches, which make changing bulbs a snap.

Imagine yourself grilling on the patio, welcoming evening guests or just gazing at the summer stars—all in the soft glow of these unobtrusive sentinels.

Whether you decide to make one light post or several, this easy-to-build project will provide years of enjoyment for both family and guests.

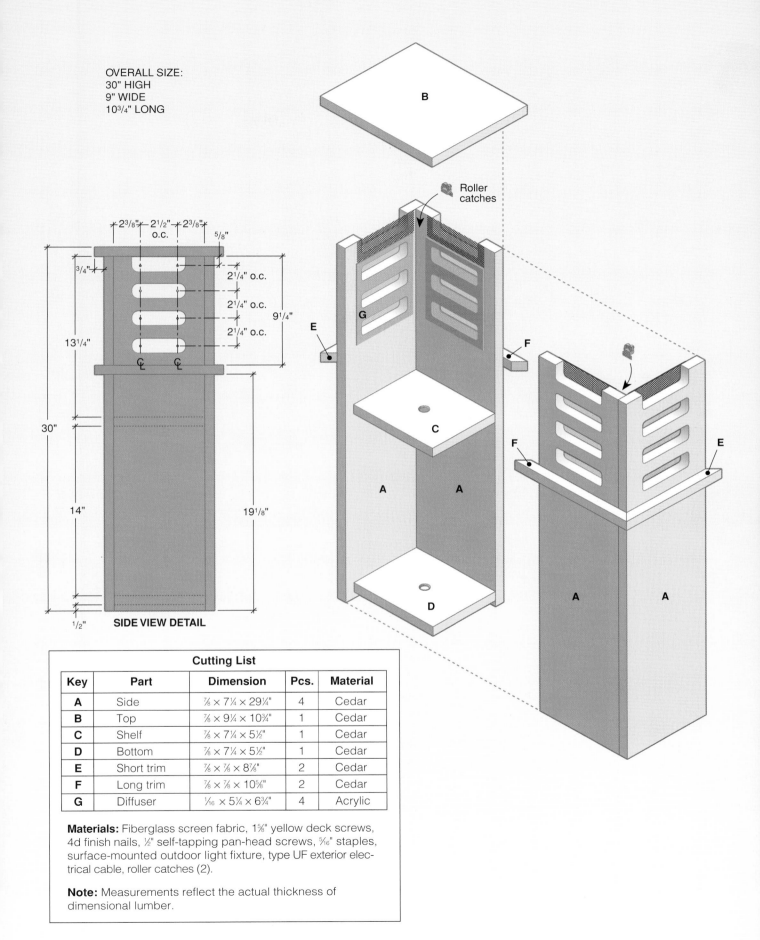

OVERALL SIZE:
30" HIGH
9" WIDE
10 3/4" LONG

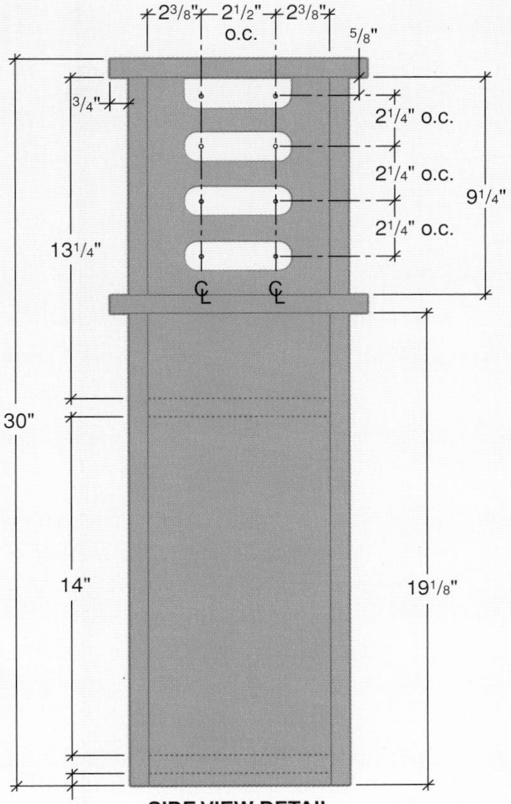
2 3/8"
2 1/2" o.c.
2 3/8"
5/8"
3/4"
2 1/4" o.c.
2 1/4" o.c.
2 1/4" o.c.
9 1/4"
13 1/4"
30"
14"
19 1/8"
1/2"

SIDE VIEW DETAIL

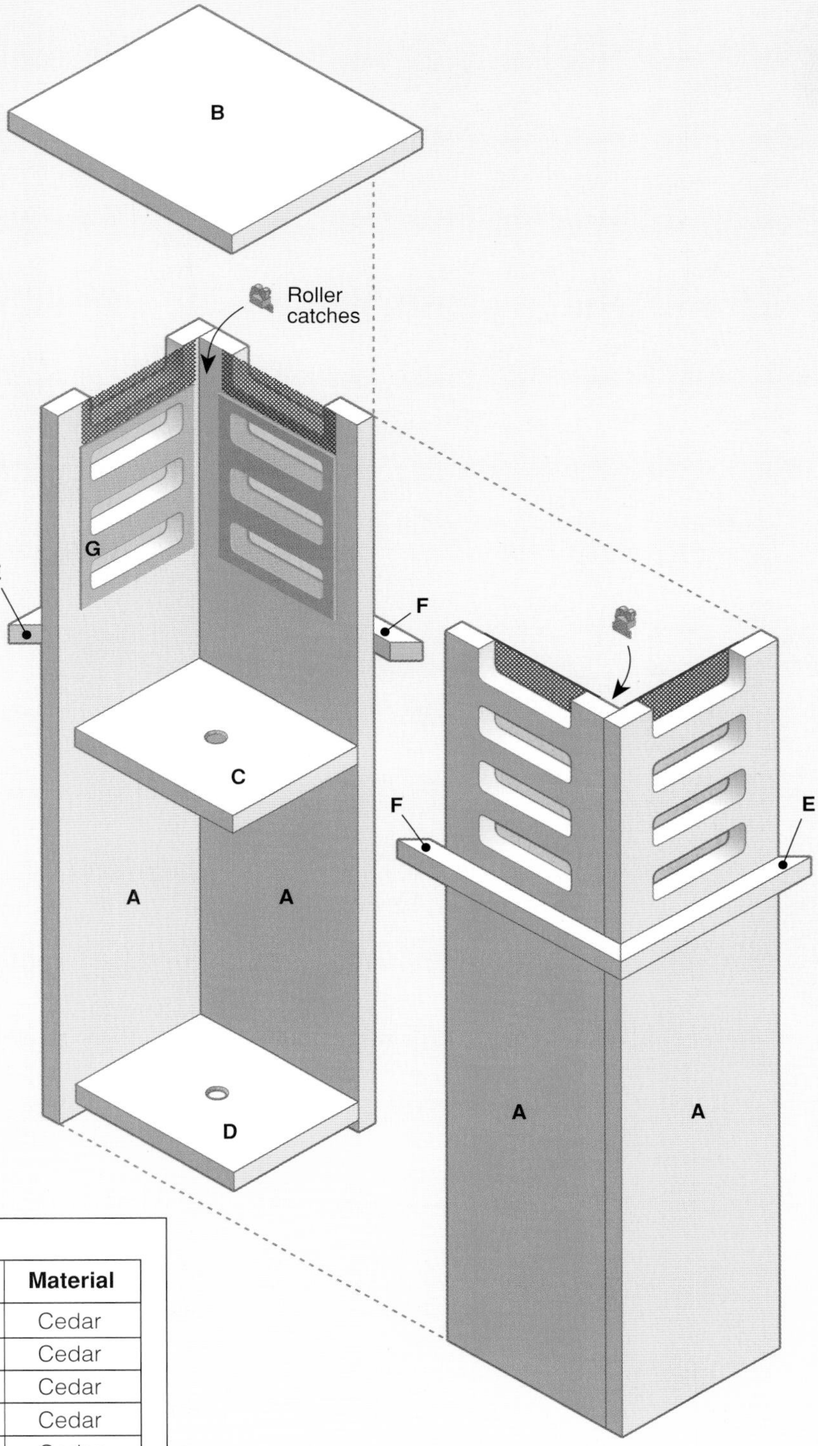
B
Roller catches
G
E
F
C
A
A
D
F
E
A
A

Cutting List				
Key	**Part**	**Dimension**	**Pcs.**	**Material**
A	Side	⅞ × 7¼ × 29¼"	4	Cedar
B	Top	⅞ × 9¼ × 10¾"	1	Cedar
C	Shelf	⅞ × 7¼ × 5½"	1	Cedar
D	Bottom	⅞ × 7¼ × 5½"	1	Cedar
E	Short trim	⅞ × ⅞ × 8⅞"	2	Cedar
F	Long trim	⅞ × ⅞ × 10⅝"	2	Cedar
G	Diffuser	1⁄16 × 5¼ × 6¾"	4	Acrylic

Materials: Fiberglass screen fabric, 1⅝" yellow deck screws, 4d finish nails, ½" self-tapping pan-head screws, 5⁄16" staples, surface-mounted outdoor light fixture, type UF exterior electrical cable, roller catches (2).

Note: Measurements reflect the actual thickness of dimensional lumber.

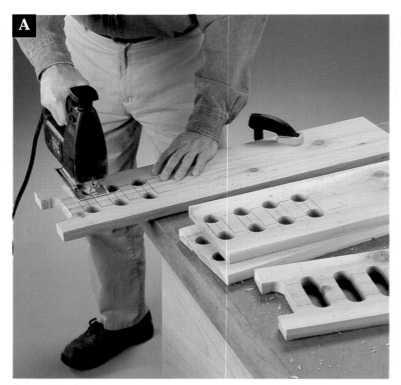

Create the diffuser and screen openings by drilling the ends with a 1¼" spade bit and completing the cuts with your jig saw.

Attach the diffusers with pan-head screws, taking care not to fracture the acrylic.

Directions:
Exterior Light Post

MAKE THE SIDES. Cedar lumber typically comes ⅞" thick, with one side planed smooth and the other side left rough. For this project we turned the smooth side out.

Start by cutting the sides (A) to length from 1 × 8 boards.

Mark the centerpoints for the holes that will become the openings for the diffusers and screens (see *Diagram*). Drill the holes with a 1¼" spade bit. Draw lines to connect the pairs of holes, and use your jig saw to cut along the lines and complete the openings **(photo A).** Sand the insides of the openings with a 1" drum sander mounted on your drill;

a light touch here will yield best results because of the softness of cedar wood.

To cut the diffusers, mark cutting lines on acrylic, then score the lines using a utility knife and metal straightedge. Then, snap the acrylic at the lines.

Position a diffuser over the lower three openings on each side piece and drill screw holes very slowly with a ⅟₁₆" bit (a special bit for drilling plastic is recommended but not essential). Mount each diffuser with ½" self-tapping pan-head screws **(photo B).** After the diffusers are attached, cut the screens to size and fasten over the top openings with ⁵⁄₁₆" staples **(photo C).**

Mark the locations of the shelf and bottom on the inner faces of the four sides **(photo D).** Flip the sides over and measure down from the top edges to mark the locations of the trim

pieces on the outer faces.

Next, drill countersunk pilot holes along both edges of two sides. Fasten three sides together with deck screws.

CUT AND INSTALL THE SHELF, BOTTOM AND TOP. Double-check the actual dimensions of your project, then cut the shelf (C) and bottom (D) to size. Using a spade bit, drill a ¾" hole for the electrical cable in the center of both pieces. Position the shelf and bottom in place, drill countersunk pilot holes and secure with deck screws. Attach a generous length (3 to 4') of UF exterior electrical cable to the fixture and mount the fixture in the center of the shelf. Feed the wire through the bottom **(photo E).**

Cut the top (B) to size from 1 × 10 stock, and center it on the partially assembled light post. Position and install the roller catches.

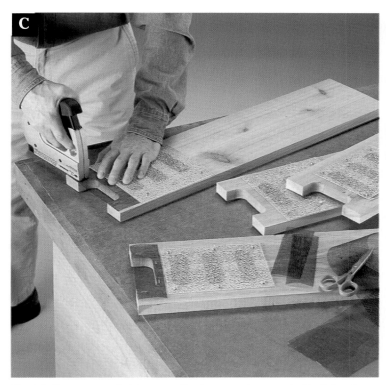

Stretch the screens tight across the top openings and attach in place with ⁵⁄₁₆" staples.

Measure up from the bottom edge to mark positions of the shelf, bottom and trim pieces.

COMPLETE THE ASSEMBLY. Screw the remaining side in place. Cut the trim pieces (E, F), mitering the corners. Drill pilot holes and attach the trim pieces to the light post with 4d galvanized finish nails.

APPLY THE FINISHING TOUCHES. Sand the surfaces and break the edges with medium-grit sandpaper. One of the benefits of cedar for outdoor projects is that it doesn't require a finish. It will, however, quickly develop a weathered appearance unless an exterior stain or clear exterior finish is applied.

INSTALLATION. Unless you have considerable experience with electrical projects, hire an electrician to run wiring to your light post. If you decide to do this work yourself, make sure to check on local Code restrictions. One option for mounting the light post in your yard is to attach a ¾" pipe flange and

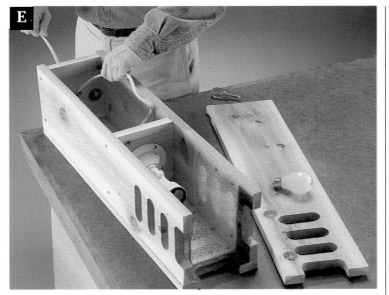

Pull the electrical cable from the fixture through the ¾" hole in the bottom of the light post.

an 18" length of galvanized pipe to the bottom of the light post, and embed the pipe in firmly packed earth or a concrete footing.

Prairie Windmill

With a mill section that turns and spins in the wind, this lively little windmill becomes the focal point of any garden.

Modeled loosely after the old turn-of-the-century windmills that dotted the prairie landscape, this fun, active garden accent may be just the thing to put some spice into your yard. With a solid, staked base firmly planted on the ground, this windmill spins and turns with the passing breezes.

We used cedar siding for the blades and tail of the mill section. The beveled cedar is the perfect shape and weight for catching the wind, and, because it's cedar, it will withstand the elements. The moving parts spin on lag screws and nylon washers, which perform better with moving parts than metal washers.

Overall, the most impressive part of this prairie windmill may be the geometrically strik-ing tower section, which rises from the base to anchor the spinning mill above. Despite its size, the tower section is very easy to make. You can set the completed windmill in the heart of your garden, or posi-tion it in a corner of your yard to create a unique accent. Ei-ther way, you won't be disap-pointed. This is a fun project, and you'll get a glowing sense of satisfaction when you see it spinning and turning in the wind like a real windmill—just the way you built it.

CONSTRUCTION MATERIALS

Quantity	Lumber
2	4 × 4" × 6' cedar
1	2 × 10" × 6' cedar
1	2 × 6" × 6' cedar
1	2 × 4" × 6' cedar
5	2 × 2" × 8' cedar
1	⅜ × 7" × 6' cedar siding
2	¾"-dia. × 3' hardwood dowel

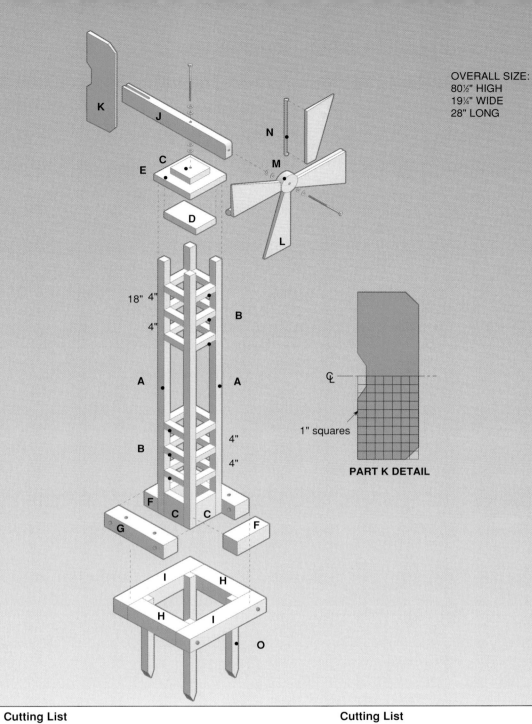

OVERALL SIZE:
80½" HIGH
19¼" WIDE
28" LONG

18" 4"

4"

B

A   A

B

4"

4"

F

C   C

G

F

I   H

H   I

O

PART K DETAIL

1" squares

Key	Part	Dimension	Pcs.	Material
A	Post	1½ × 1½ × 60"	4	Cedar
B	Rail	1½ × 1½ × 5"	24	Cedar
C	Spacer	1½ × 5 × 5"	5	Cedar
D	Top insert	1½ × 5 × 8"	1	Cedar
E	Top	1½ × 9¼ × 9¼"	1	Cedar
F	Base end	3½ × 3½ × 8"	2	Cedar
G	Base side	3½ × 3½ × 15"	2	Cedar
H	Foot end	3½ × 3½ × 12"	2	Cedar

Key	Part	Dimension	Pcs.	Material
I	Foot side	3½ × 3½ × 19"	2	Cedar
J	Shaft	1½ × 3½ × 26½"	1	Cedar
K	Tail	⅝ × 7 × 24"	1	Cedar siding
L	Blade	⅝ × 7 × 12"	4	Cedar siding
M	Hub	1½ × 4 × 4"	1	Cedar
N	Backer rod	¾ × ¾ × 13"	4	Dowel
O	Stake	1½ × 1½ × 18"	4	Cedar

Cutting List

Materials: Moisture-resistant glue, epoxy glue, lag screws (⅜ × 6", ⅜ × 8"), deck screws (1¼", 2½", 3"), panhead screws (#4 × 1"), 1"-dia. nylon washers, finishing materials.

Note: Measurements reflect the actual size of dimensional lumber.

Directions:
Prairie Windmill

BUILD THE TOWER FRAME. The main frame for the windmill tower is made up of four posts connected by a series of short rails. Cut the posts (A) and rails (B). Clamp all four posts in a row, and mark the rail locations on all the posts, starting 9" up from one end of the posts and following the spacing shown in the *Diagram* on page 95. Unclamp the posts, and arrange them in pairs. Attach the rails between the posts at the location marks to create two ladderlike assemblies. Use moisture-resistant glue and a single countersunk 2½" deck screw, driven through each post and into each rail. Once the two assemblies are completed, join them together with rails to create the tower frame.

ADD THE TOWER BOTTOM & TOP. Cut the spacers (C), top insert (D), and tower top (E) to size. Four of the spacers are installed between the posts at the bottom of the tower, and the fifth is mounted on top of the tower. Fit four of the spacers between the posts at the bottom, and attach them with glue and 2½" deck screws driven through countersunk pilot holes. On the fifth spacer, draw diagonal lines between opposite corners—the point where the lines intersect is the center of the board. Center the spacer on the tower top (E), and attach it with glue and 1¼" deck screws. Do not drive screws within 1" of the centerpoint. Drill a ¼"-dia. pilot hole for a ⅜"-dia. lag screw through the center, making sure to keep your drill perpendicular—the lag screw is driven later to

secure the windmill to the tower. Next, slip the top insert between the posts at the top of the tower, and fasten the insert with glue and screws. Complete the tower top by centering the spacer and tower top over the top insert and fastening with glue and screws. After assembly is complete, use a power sander to smooth out all sharp edges **(photo A).**

ATTACH THE TOWER BASE. The base of the tower is a heavy frame made from 4 × 4 cedar. When the windmill is installed in your yard, the base is attached to a 4 × 4 frame that is staked into the ground. Cut the base ends (F) and base sides (G) to size. Attach the base ends to the tower with 3" deck screws. To attach the base sides, drill ¼"-dia. pilot holes for ⅜"-dia. lag screws in the base sides, then counterbore the pilot holes with a 1" spade bit. Drive ⅜ × 8" lag screws with metal washers through the base sides and into the base ends. Cut the foot end (H) and foot side (I) to size. Drill pilot holes for counterbored lag screws through the the foot sides, and secure each foot side to the foot ends with a ⅜ × 8" lag screw.

MAKE THE TAIL. Cut the tail (K) to length from beveled cedar lap siding. Draw a 1" grid pattern onto the board, then

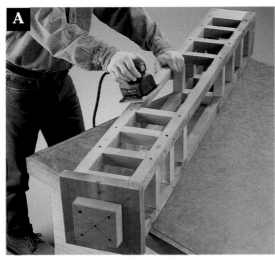

A

The tower for the windmill is basically two ladder frames joined by rails. Sand sharp edges smooth.

draw the shape shown in the *Part K Detail*, page 95. Make sure the notch is on the thick edge. Cut with a jig saw.

MAKE THE SHAFT. Cut the shaft (J) to size from a cedar 2 × 4. Draw a centerline on one long edge of the shaft. Cut a slot into the end of the shaft to hold the tail: first, measure the thickness of the beveled siding at several points, including the thin edge and the thick edge. Using drill bits with the same diameters as the thicknesses of the siding, drill holes along the centerline at points that correspond with the width of the tail—make sure that you drill holes at each end of the slot outline. Connect the holes with a pair of straight lines to create an outline for the tail notch. Cut along the outlines with a handsaw **(photo B).** Next, drill a centered, ⁷⁄₁₆"-dia. guide hole (for the lag screw that secures the shaft to the tower) through the top edge of the shaft, 9" from the front end. Also drill a ¼"-dia. pilot hole in the center of the front end of the shaft.

MAKE THE BLADES & HUB. Cut the propeller blades (L)

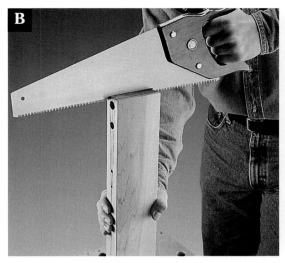

Drill holes of varying diameter to create an outline, then cut a slot for the tail into the shaft.

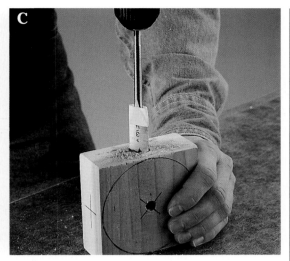

Drill ¾"-dia. × 1"-deep guide holes into the four sides of the hub to hold the backer rods.

and hub (M) to the full sizes listed in the *Cutting List*. On the thin edge of each blade board, draw a cutting line so the blade tapers from 7" in width at one end to 2" in width at the other end. Cut the blades to shape with a circular saw. To make the circular hub, first draw diagonal lines between opposite corners on the face of the hub board. Set the point of a compass at the intersection point of the diagonal lines, and draw a circle with a 2" radius. Drill a ⁷⁄₁₆"-dia. hole through the centerpoint. Then mark drilling points on all four edges of the hub board, centered end to end and side to side, for drilling the holes that will hold the backer rods. Install a ¾"-dia. spade bit in your drill, then wrap a piece of masking tape 1" up from the bottom of the cutting part of the bit. Use the masking tape as a guide for stopping the holes when they reach 1" in depth. Drill ¾"-dia. × 1"-deep holes at the centerpoints in each edge of the hub board **(photo C).** Cut out the hub with a jig saw, following the round cutting line. Cut the

backer rods (N) from ¾" doweling, then sand a flat edge onto each rod, using a belt sander. Stop the flat edges 1" from the end of each dowel (this creates a flat mounting surface).

ASSEMBLE THE PROPELLER. Attach the thick edge of each blade to the flat surface of a backer rod with three #4 × 1" panhead screws and epoxy glue **(photo D).** Apply epoxy glue to the tail where it meets the shaft, and fasten it in the slot with 1¼" deck screws. Before proceeding, apply exterior wood stain to all the wood parts, and apply paste wax in the guide holes in the hub and shaft. Attach the blade assembly to the shaft with a ⅜ × 6" lag screw and pairs of 1"-dia. nylon washers inserted on each side of the hub. Fasten the shaft to the tower with a ⅜ × 6" lag screw and pairs of nylon

washers at the top and bottom edges of the shaft. Do not over-tighten the screws.

SET UP THE WINDMILL. Position the 4 × 4 frame in the desired location in your yard or garden. Cut the stakes (O), sharpening one end of each stake. Attach the stakes at the inside corners of the foot frame with screws, then drive the stakes into the ground. Attach the base frame to the foot frame with counterbored lag screws. Drive counterbored lag screws through the base sides and into the foot ends.

Glue the ends of the backer rods into the holes in the hub to mount the propeller blades.

Sundial

This throwback to ancient times casts a shadow of classical elegance in your yard or garden— and it tells time, too.

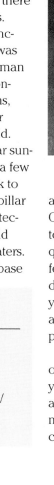

Sundials have been popular garden accessories for just about as long as there have been formal gardens. While their time-telling function is not as critical as it was around the time of the Roman Empire, sundials today continue to dot formal gardens, and even suburban flower beds, throughout the world.

The design for the cedar sundial shown here contains a few elements that harken back to ancient times. The fluted pillar suggests the famous architectural columns of Old World cathedrals and amphitheaters. The plates at the top and base are trimmed with a Roman Ogee router bit for a Classical touch. Making these cuts requires a router and several different types of router bits. If you don't mind a little plainer look, you can bypass the router work and simply round over the parts with a power sander.

This sundial is not just another stylish accent for your yard or garden. You can actually use it to tell time. Simply mount the triangular shadow-caster (called a "gnomon") to the face of the sundial, and orient it so it points north. Then calibrate the face at twelve hourly intervals. That way you know that the positioning of the numbers is accurate.

This sundial is secured to the ground with a post anchor that fits around a mounting block on the underside of the sundial. The anchor is driven into the ground, making it easy to move the sundial (you'll appreciate this the first time Daylight Savings Time comes around).

CONSTRUCTION MATERIALS

Quantity	Lumber
1	1 × 12" × 4' cedar
1	6 × 6" × 4' cedar
1	4 × 4" × 4' cedar
1	⅜ × 10 × 10" ceramic tile/ marble
1	¼ × 11 × 12" plexiglass

OVERALL SIZE:
40⅛" HIGH
11¼" WIDE
11¼" LONG

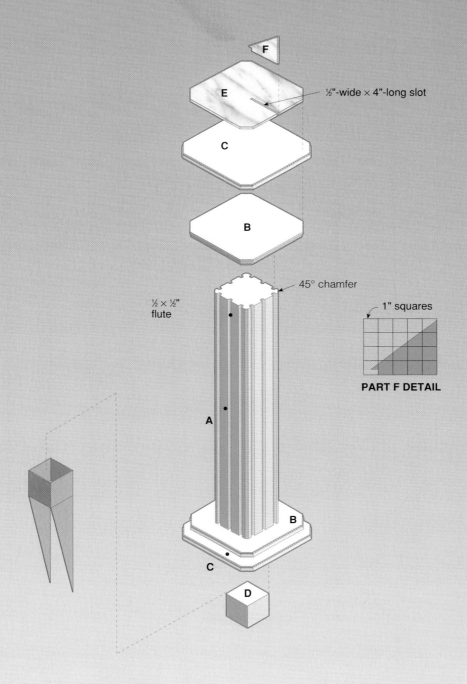

½"-wide × 4"-long slot

½ × ½"
flute

45° chamfer

1" squares

PART F DETAIL

Cutting List				
Key	**Part**	**Dimension**	**Pcs.**	**Material**
A	Column	5½ × 5½ × 32¾"	1	Cedar
B	Inner plate	⅞ × 10 × 10"	2	Cedar
C	Outer plate	⅞ × 11¼ × 11¼"	2	Cedar

Cutting List				
Key	**Part**	**Dimension**	**Pcs.**	**Material**
D	Mounting block	3½ × 3½ × 3"	1	Cedar
E	Dial face	⅜ × 10 × 10"	1	Ceramic tile
F	Gnomon	¼ × 3⅞ × 4½"	1	Plexiglass

Materials: 1¼", 2" galvanized deck screws, construction adhesive, silicone caulk, clock-face numbers, 4 × 4 metal post anchor.

Note: Measurements reflect the actual thickness of dimensional lumber.

Directions: Sundial

MAKE THE COLUMN. Cut the column from a 6 × 6" cedar post, then use a router to make the decorative grooves (called flutes) that run up and down the post. Start the column construction by cutting the column (A) to length from a 4'-long 6 × 6" cedar post. Next, use a combination square as a marking gauge to lay out three pairs of parallel lines lengthwise on each face of the column —the lines in each pair should be ½" apart **(photo A).** These lines form the outlines for the fluted grooves that will be cut into the post. The two outer-flute outlines should start ¾"

from the edge, and the middle flute should be 1¼" from each outer outline. Install a ½" core box bit in your router—a core box bit is a straight bit with a rounded bottom. Hook the edge guide on the foot of your router over the edge of the post (or, use a straightedge cutting guide to guide the router), and cut each ½"-deep flute in two passes. After all 12 flutes are cut, install a 45° chamfering bit in your router and trim off all four edges of the column **(photo B).**

CUT THE FLAT PARTS. Two flat, square boards are sandwiched together and attached at the top and bottom of the column. The boards are trimmed at the corners to mimic the shape of the floor tile we used for the sundial face, and they also feature decorative edges cut with a router. Cut the inner plates (B) and outer plates (C) to

size from 1 × 12 cedar. After the plates are cut to final size, trim off a corner with 1" legs from all four corners of each plate, using a jig saw **(photo C).** Install a piloted bit in your router to cut edge contours (we used a double ogee fillet bit), then cut the roundovers on all edges of the plates **(photo D).**

MAKE THE SUNDIAL FACE. We used a piece of octagonal marble floor tile for the face of our sundial. If you prefer, you can use inexpensive ceramic floor tile instead of marble, but either way you should purchase a piece of tile that is already cut to the correct size and shape for the project (cutting floor tile is very difficult). The shadow-caster, or gnomon, is cut from plexiglass, and inserted into a slot in the marble. Lay out the ¼"-wide, 4"-long slot for the gnomon, centered on one edge of the sundial face. Have the slot cut at a tile shop (if this is a problem, you are probably better off eliminating the slot than trying to cut it yourself). Next, mark a 1"-square grid pattern on a small piece of ¼"-thick white plexiglass. Lay out the shape and dimensions of the gnomon,

Lay out three ½"-wide flutes on each column face using a combination square as a marking gauge.

Trim off the corners of the column with a router and a 45° chamfering bit.

Cut triangular cutoffs with 1" legs at each corner of each plate.

Cut decorative profiles along the edges of the inner and outer plates.

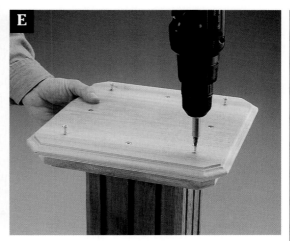

Make sure screws driven through the outer plate are at least 2" in from the edges.

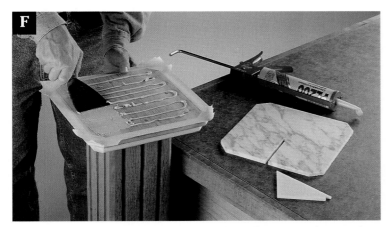

Frame the top of the top outer plate with masking tape, then apply a layer of construction adhesive to attach the sundial face.

following the *Grid Pattern* (F) on page 99. Mount a wood-cutting blade with medium-size teeth in your jig saw, and cut the gnomon shape. Sand the edges with 100-grit sandpaper, then finish-sand with fine paper, up to 180-or 220-grit. Fit the gnomon into the slot on the sundial face.

ASSEMBLE THE SUNDIAL. Attach an inner plate, centered, to each end of the column, using 2½" deck screws. Cut the mounting block (D) to length from 4 × 4 cedar (or two pieces of cedar 2 × 4). Attach the block to one face of the bottom outer plate, centered, using

deck screws driven through the plate and into the block. Do not attach the base plate to the column assembly yet. Attach the top outer plate to the top inner plate, making sure the overhang is equal on all four sides and the corners align **(photo E).** Set the post on its base, and attach the sundial face to the top outer plate, using construction adhesive **(photo F).** Make sure the face is centered and in alignment. Place construction adhesive into the gnomon slot, then insert the gnomon into the slot and press firmly. Seal all joints around the edges of the gnomon and the edges of the

face, using clear silicone caulk. Attach the bottom outer plate by laying the column on its side and driving 1¼" deck screws up through the outer plate and into the inner plate. Coat wood parts with exterior wood stain.

INSTALL & CALIBRATE THE SUN-DIAL. Choose a sunny spot to install your sundial. Lay a piece of scrap wood on the spot, pointing directly north (use a magnetic compass for reference). Purchase a metal post anchor for a 4 × 4 post (most have an attached metal stake about 18" long). Drive the post anchor (G) into the ground at the desired location, making sure one side of the box part of the anchor is perpendicular to the scrap piece facing north. Insert the mounting block on the base of the post into the anchor, making sure the gnomon is facing north. To calibrate the sundial, mark a point at the edge of the shadow from the gnomon at the top of every hour. Apply hour markers at those points. We used metal Roman numerals from a craft store, attached with clear silicone caulk.

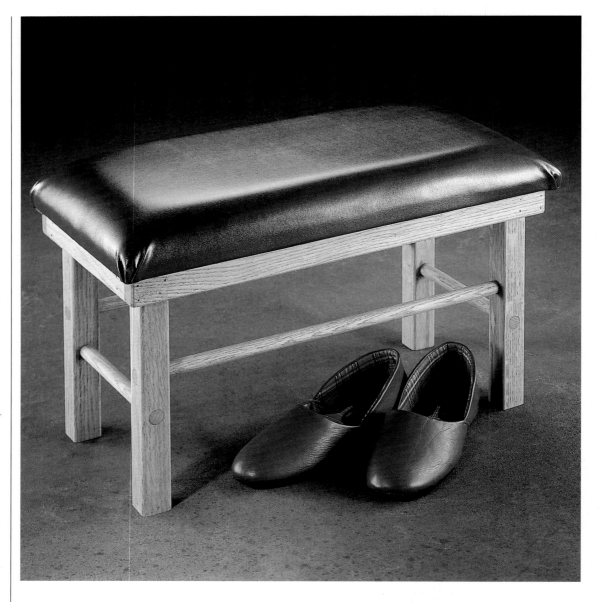

Oak Footstool

*Rugged simplicity is the hallmark of this versatile
and easy-to-build oak footstool.*

Quantity	Lumber
1	2 × 2" × 8' red oak
1	1 × 2" × 6' red oak
1	¾" × 2 × 4' plywood
2	¾"-dia. × 3' oak dowels

This simple footstool features rugged construction and adaptable styling so it can blend into nearly any den or family room. Select an upholstery style that works with your decor, and this footstool will look as if it was custom-made just for your room.

The support framework is made of solid red oak, with oak through-dowel stringers that give it a subtle design touch.

Call it a footstool, an ottoman or even a hassock. Use it to rest and elevate your tired feet, or employ it as extra seating in front of your television. Whatever you call it and however you use it, this oak footstool will quickly become one of your most useful furnishings.

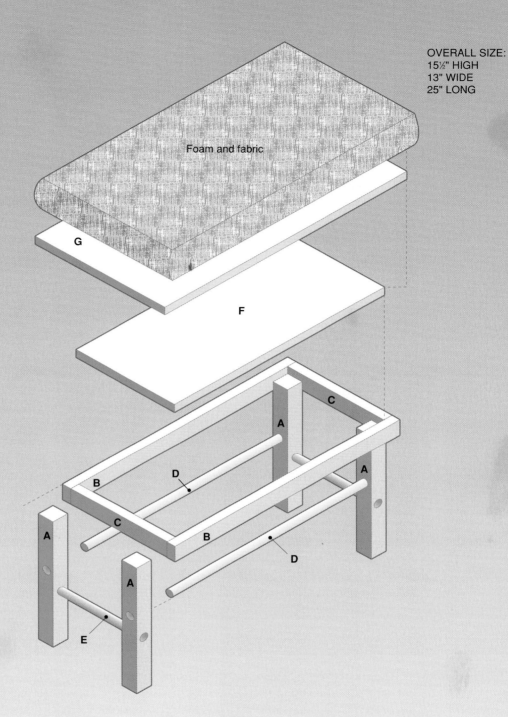

OVERALL SIZE:
15½" HIGH
13" WIDE
25" LONG

Foam and fabric

G

F

C

A

B

D

A

A

B

C

D

A

A

E

Cutting List				
Key	**Part**	**Dimension**	**Pcs.**	**Material**
A	Leg	1½ × 1½ × 12"	4	Red oak
B	Apron	¾ × 1½ × 24"	2	Red oak
C	Apron	¾ × 1½ × 10½"	2	Red oak
D	Stringer	¾"-dia. × 22½"	2	Oak dowel

Cutting List				
Key	**Part**	**Dimension**	**Pcs.**	**Material**
E	Stringer	¾"-dia. × 10½"	2	Oak dowel
F	Top	¾ × 10½ × 22½"	1	Plywood
G	Seat board	¾ × 13 × 25"	1	Plywood

Materials: 6d brass-plate finish nails, #6 × 1¼" brass wood screws, 2 × 13 × 25" high-density foam rubber, 19 × 31" upholstery fabric, upholstery tacks, rubber glides or tack-on chair glides (4), finishing materials.

Note: Measurements reflect the actual thickness of dimensional lumber.

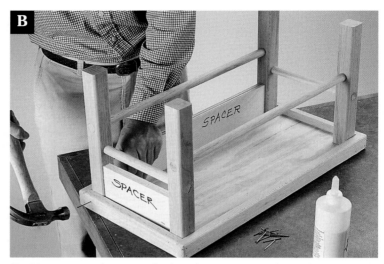

With the legs taped in a square bundle, use a drill and a portable drill guide to make the dowel holes.

Position spacers between the legs for support, and attach the apron to the leg assembly.

Directions: Oak Footstool

MAKE THE LEGS. All four legs for the footstool can be cut from one 8'-long oak 2 × 2. Before you cut the individual legs to length, round over the edges of the 8' board with a router and ¼" roundover bit, or with a power sander. Cut the legs (A) to length. Bundle them together edge to edge to form a square, and wrap masking tape around the bundle to hold it together. Mark and drill dowel holes for the through-dowel stringers: on one side, measure in 5" from the ends of the 2 × 2s, and draw a reference line across both exposed faces. Mark drilling points at the center of the reference line on each face. Drill through the drilling point with a ¾" spade bit (set the block on a piece of scrapwood to prevent drill tearout). Use a portable drill guide to make sure the hole is perpendicular **(photo A).** Next, give the bundle of legs a quarter turn, and draw a reference line on the exposed faces 5" in from the other end of the leg bundle. Mark centered drilling

points and drill ¾" dowel holes at each point. Remove the tape from the legs, and sand the drill bit entry and exit points until smooth.

BUILD THE APRONS. The aprons for the footstool are cut from oak 1 × 2, and attached at the tops of the legs to create a ¾"-deep recess for the plywood top. Round over an 8'-long oak 1 × 2, then cut the aprons (B, C) to length. Sand the ends smooth. Cut the top (F) to use as a spacer for attaching the aprons. Set the top on your worksurface, then wrap the top with the apron pieces so the ends of the longer aprons (B) are flush with the outer faces of the shorter aprons (C). Fasten the aprons together with glue and 6d brass-plated finish nails driven through pilot holes at each joint.

BUILD THE LEG ASSEMBLY. The leg assembly is built by attaching the legs with dowel stretchers and then fastening the assembly to the apron. Set the legs on your worksurface, making sure the legs are arranged so the dowel holes are aligned correctly (see *Dia-*

gram, page 103). Cut the stringers (D, E) to length from ¾" oak doweling. Sand the ends smooth. Dry-fit the stringers in the dowel holes. Poke each stringer end back out through each dowel hole an inch or two, then apply wood glue to the end of the stringer. Make sure all stringer ends are glued and flush with the outer faces of the legs, then reinforce each joint by driving 6d finish nails through the legs and into the ends of the stringers. Sand to make sure the dowel ends are flush with the legs. Set the legs on the top board, at the corners of the apron frame. Use spacer blocks cut from scrap to fit exactly between the leg pairs, holding them so they are perpendicular to the apron. Attach the legs to the frame with 6d finish nails and glue **(photo B).**

APPLY THE FINISH. Finish-sand the footstool frame, with 180- or 220-grit sandpaper. Wipe down with mineral spirits, and allow the wood to dry completely. Apply wood coloring agent: we used two coats of rub-on black walnut stain.

Staple the upholstery to the back of the seat board, making sure it is even and taut.

Attach the upholstered top board by driving 1¼" screws up through the seat board.

the good side facing down. Center the seat board (foam-side down) onto the back of the material. Press down lightly and evenly on the board, then pull up one end of the material and tack it to the seat board with a staple gun. Pull up the opposite end, tugging on the material until it is taut. Tack the end **(photo C).** Tuck in the corners, and tack the remaining edges in place the same way. Turn the seat board over and inspect your work. If you aren't happy with it, it's easy to redo it at this point. Once the upholstery is tacked on to your satisfaction, fasten the edges to the seat board with upholstery tacks spaced at 2" intervals.

INSTALL THE SEAT. Set the plywood top (F) into the recess at the top of the apron frame. Drill pilot holes, and attach the top to the legs with #6 × 1⅝" wood screws. Make sure the top of the board is flush with the top of the apron frame. Lay the upholstered seat facedown on a clean, flat worksurface. Invert the leg assembly, and position it over the underside of the seat board. Make sure the overhang is equal on all sides, drill pilot holes, and drive #6 × 1¼" wood screws through the top board and into the seat board around the perimeter of the board **(photo D).**

Apply a topcoat: we used three coats of rub-on tung oil. Tack chair glides to the bottom of each leg.

MAKE THE SEAT. The soft, upholstered footstool seat extends past the edges of the frame slightly. We used dark brown leather upholstery tacked onto the seat board over 2"-thick high-density foam rubber. Choose any style of upholstery that blends with your room furnishings, but make sure to use upholstery fabric. Cut the seat board (G) to size, and sand the edges smooth. Cut the 2"-thick foam rubber to the same dimensions as the seat board. To keep the foam from shifting as you attach the upholstery, tack it to the seat board with double-edge carpet tape or spray-mount adhesive. Cut the upholstery so it is large enough to extend at least 3" past each seat board edge. Lay the material on a clean, flat surface with

Candlesticks

Place these candlesticks on a table, windowsill or mantel, and watch them light up your life.

CONSTRUCTION MATERIALS

Quantity	Lumber
1	½" × 1 × 2' Baltic birch plywood
1	1 × 6" × 2' birch

We considered a wide variety of shapes and styles before deciding on this handsome design for our candlesticks. More than 11" tall, these candlesticks are both elegant and inexpensive.

Appearances can be deceiving. These candlesticks look like the work of a highly skilled woodworker, but in reality they are quite simple to build. The shaped pedestals follow a simple pattern that can be transferred to your workpiece and then cut with a jig saw. The smooth edges on the bases and tops are made with a router table and a roundover bit. A handy jig simplifies the task of attaching the pedestals to the bases. And "candle nails" hold the candles in place.

Made from inexpensive Baltic birch plywood, these candlesticks can be painted with any decorative finish you choose.

OVERALL SIZE:
11½" HIGH
5" DIAMETER

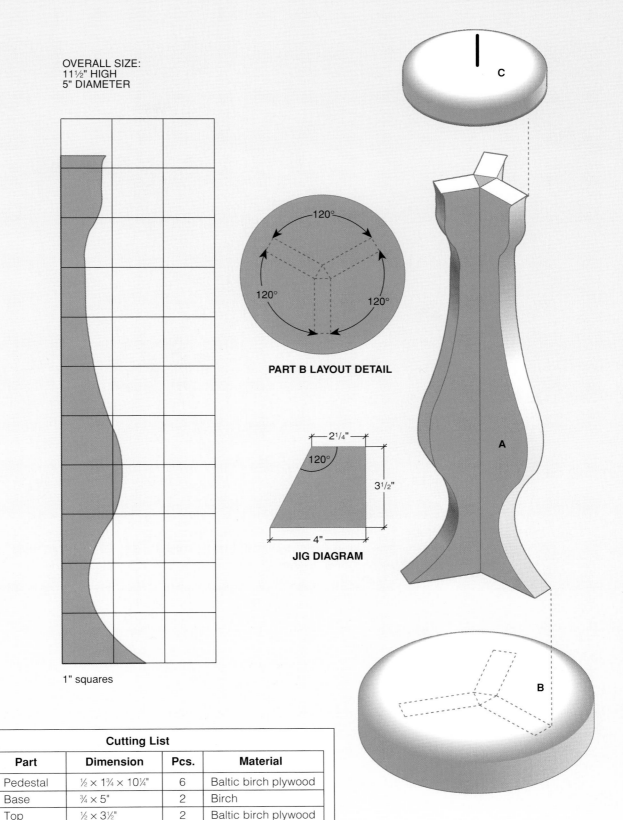

PART B LAYOUT DETAIL

JIG DIAGRAM

1" squares

Cutting List				
Key	**Part**	**Dimension**	**Pcs.**	**Material**
A	Pedestal	½ × 1¾ × 10¼"	6	Baltic birch plywood
B	Base	¾ × 5"	2	Birch
C	Top	½ × 3½"	2	Baltic birch plywood

Materials: Wood glue, wood screws (#8 × 1½"), 1" brads, 1¼" roofing nails, finishing materials.

Note: Measurements reflect the actual thickness of dimensional lumber.

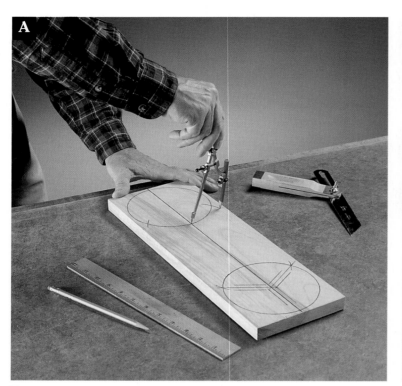

A

B

Use a compass to lay out the bases and mark the positions of the pedestals on the bases. Use a sliding T-bevel to make sure the angles are uniform.

Sand the edges of the bases with a belt sander and nail jig.

Directions: Candlesticks

MAKE THE BASES. Laying out the bases and the pedestal locations requires some basic geometry and the use of a drafting compass. Practice on paper until you're confident you understand the technique.

Start by drawing a center reference line down the length of a piece of 1 × 6" birch. Use a compass to draw two 2½"-radius circles, with centerpoints positioned on the reference line.

With the compass still set at 2½", place the tip at one of the points where the reference line crosses the circle, and scribe two arcs intersecting the circle. Draw lines connecting each of these intersection points to the centerpoint of the circle. These lines, along with the original reference line, form the three centerlines for the pedestal pieces. To mark the outline of the pedestal pieces, draw parallel lines ¼" on each side of the three centerlines. Repeat this process for the other circle **(photo A).** Use a jig saw to cut out the bases (B).

Build a sanding jig from a scrap piece of ¾" wood. Drill a pilot hole no more than 1½" from the end of the scrap board. Also drill a pilot hole through the centerpoint of the base. Drive a 1¾" nail through the pilot hole in the jig and into the base. Clamp a belt sander perpendicular to your worksurface and sand the edge of the base by rotating it on the nail **(photo B).** Repeat for the other base.

MAKE THE TOPS AND SHAPE THE PIECES. Use a compass set to 1¾" radius to draw two circles on ½" Baltic birch, and cut out the tops (C) with a jig saw. To sand the edges of each top, drill pilot holes through the centerpoint and use the nail jig and your belt sander.

Using a router table and a ¼" roundover bit, shape both edges of the tops and the top edges of the bases **(photo C).**

BUILD AND ATTACH THE PEDESTALS. Build the placement jig (see *Diagram*) to use as a guide when positioning the pedestal pieces.

Cut the pedestal blanks (A) to size. Transfer the pattern (see *Diagram*) to the blanks and cut with a jig saw. Clamp the pieces together, attach a drum sander to your drill and gang-sand the edges of the pedestals.

TIP

When transferring a grid pattern, you have two options. You can enlarge the pattern on a copier and trace it onto a piece of cardboard to form a tracing template. Or, you can grid your stock with 1" squares and draw the pattern by hand directly onto the workpieces.

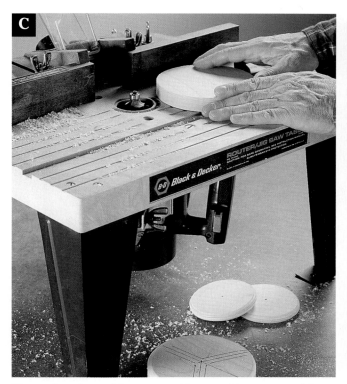

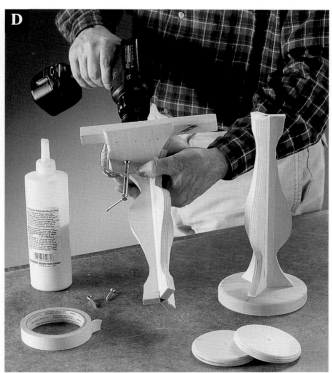

Shape the edges of the tops and bases with a router table and a ¼" piloted roundover bit.

Attach the pedestal pieces to one another with masking tape when joining them to the base.

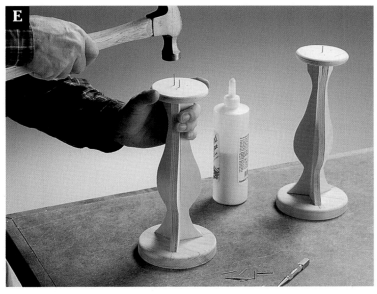

Attach the top to the pedestals with wood glue and 1" brads.

Using the pedestal outlines as a guide, drill pilot holes through the base, then countersink the holes from the bottom side. Position two pedestals on your worksurface so the back edges are against each other and the top and bottom edges are flush. Join the pedestals with a strip of masking tape. Fold the left pedestal over the right and align the third pedestal along the back edge of the left pedestal and join with tape.

Align the 120° angle of the placement jig along the outlines of two adjacent pedestal pieces, and clamp it to the base. Attach the pedestals with glue and screws driven up through the bottom face of the base, holding the pedestals firmly against the jig **(photo D).** After attaching two pedestals, reposition the jig and attach the third pedestal.

ATTACH THE TOPS. Drive a "candle nail" (we used a 1¼" roofing nail) up through the pilot hole in the center of each top. Center the tops on the pedestals, drill pilot holes and attach them with glue and 1" brads **(photo E).** Set the nail heads.

APPLY FINISHING TOUCHES. Scrape off any excess glue, and fill nail holes with putty. Finish-sand the candlesticks, and paint as desired (we used a "burled mahogany" faux paint kit).

Trivet

*Protect your countertops, tables and furniture during teatime
with our Colonial-style trivet.*

Y ou'll love this easy-to-
construct trivet. Its intri-
cate trim and arched
legs make it a popular conversation piece during teatime.

The heavy tile stabilizes the
base, making it ideal for keeping teapots off your favorite furniture or serving cart. For this
project, we selected a standard
Colonial oak trim pattern to
make the arched legs and a
neutral-color tile for the base,
but you can customize this
trivet by using any color of tile
that matches your tea set or
suits your taste. Our basic design features a single 12 × 12"
tile cut down to a finished size
of 6 × 9". Using one tile is a
simple method that doesn't

require grout. But you will find
it easy to adapt this design for
smaller tiles or mosaic tiles that
do require grout: simply match
the size of the substrate to the
finished dimensions of the tile-
and-grout surface (including a
grout border between the tiles
and the oak frame), and cut
the oak molding pieces accord-
ingly. The construction steps remain the same.

CONSTRUCTION MATERIALS

Quantity	Lumber
1	¾" × 2 × 2' MDF
1	⅝ × 2¼" × 4' oak molding
1	¼ × 12 × 12" tile

MDF = medium-density fiberboard

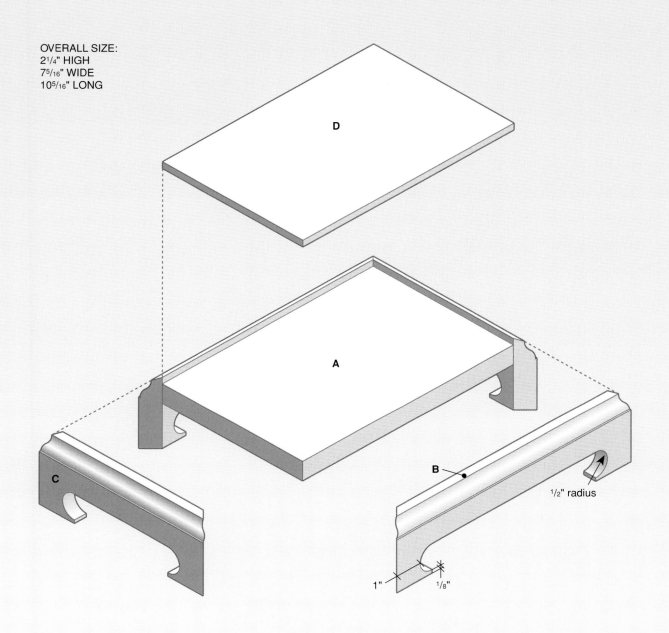

OVERALL SIZE:
2¼" HIGH
7⁵/₁₆" WIDE
10⁵/₁₆" LONG

D

A

C

B

½" radius

1"   ¹/₈"

Cutting List				
Key	**Part**	**Dimension**	**Pcs.**	**Material**
A	Substrate	¾ × 6 × 9"	1	MDF
B	Side	⅝ × 2¼ × 10⁵/₁₆"	2	Oak molding
C	End	⅝ × 2¼ × 5⁵/₁₆"	2	Oak molding
D	Tile	¼ × 6 × 9"	1	Ceramic tile

Materials: Waterproof wood glue, tile adhesive, 1" brads, finishing materials. (Optional: grout, clear silicone caulk.)

Note: Measurements reflect the actual thickness of dimensional lumber.

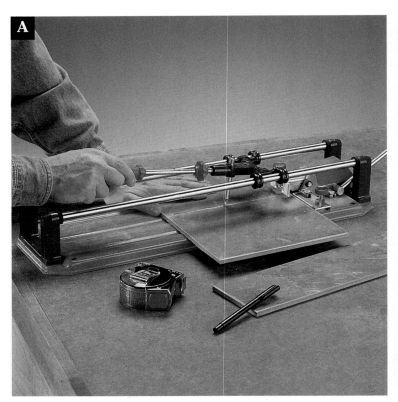

Use a tile cutter to make fast, clean cuts on ceramic tile.

Test-fit the base molding side and end pieces to the substrate and tile before applying glue.

Directions: Trivet

CUT THE TILE AND SUBSTRATE. We've found a 12 × 12" tile cut to 6 × 9" is a convenient size for a trivet. It is large enough to hold a good-sized teapot, yet small enough to handle easily. Select your tile (D), then mark and cut it to the correct size with a tile cutter **(photo A).** If you don't have a tile cutter, clamp the tile to your worksurface and cut it using a rod saw (similar to a coping saw, but with an abrasive blade designed for cutting tile). Measure and cut the substrate (A) to match the finished tile size.

CUT THE MOLDING. Cut the sides (B) and ends (C) to length from the base molding. Make 45° miter cuts at the ends of each piece.

ATTACH MOLDING TO SUBSTRATE. Place the tile facedown on the worksurface and position the substrate, bottom side up, over the tile. Test-fit each side and end against the substrate. Scribe a line along the edge of the substrate to mark where the substrate joins the molding **(photo B).** Apply waterproof glue to the sides and ends, and attach them to the substrate so the reference marks are aligned. With the tile temporarily in place, fasten a band clamp around the perimeter at the line where the substrate edges meet the base molding **(photo C).** After the glue dries, remove the band clamp and the tile. Drill pilot holes through the molding into the substrate. Secure the molding with 1" brads, and recess the nail heads with a nail set.

CREATE THE LEGS. Legs are formed by cutting holes in the molding near each corner joint. Along the bottom edges of each side and end, measure in 1½" inches from each corner and ⅝" up from the bottom edge. This is the centerpoint for each hole. Construct a small support jig/backer board to fit inside the skirt formed by the base molding. For a 6 × 9" tile inset, a 6 × 9" piece of scrap will do. Attach the jig to the bench so it overhangs the edge. Place the trivet on the jig, and drill holes at each centerpoint with a 1" spade bit **(photo D).** Be careful that you drill only through the sides and ends, and not into the substrate. Draw a connecting line between the tops of each set of

Use a band clamp to hold base and ends in contact with the substrate while glue dries.

Use scrap plywood to support trivet and prevent tearouts while drilling "leg" holes in the molding.

holes, and cut along this line with your jig saw. Complete each cutout by cutting straight up from the bottom edge into the center of each hole **(photo E).**

SAND AND FINISH. Sand the cutout edges with 150-grit sandpaper, making sure to round the sharp edges on the bottom of the legs. Finish the trivet as desired.

ATTACH THE TILE. Apply an even coat of tile adhesive to the top of the substrate, and set the tile into the base. Depending on the width of the gap between the molding and the tile on the finished piece, you may want to fill it with a clear silicone caulk to prevent moisture or crumbs from collecting. If you selected mosaic tiles for this project, mask the sides of

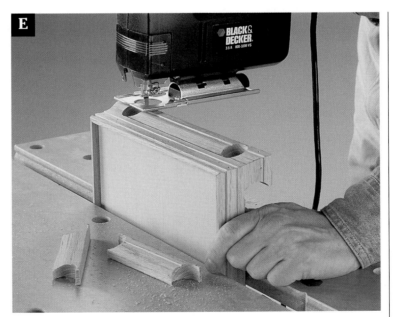

Clamp the trivet to your worksurface, and carefully cut out the legs, using a jig saw.

the base before grouting to protect the molding and apply a silicone grout sealer when fin

ished to prevent stains from penetrating the grout.

Silverware Caddy

*This decorative display rack brings convenience
to dinnertime chores.*

CONSTRUCTION MATERIALS

Quantity	Lumber
1	½ × 8" × 4' oak "hobby wood"

Silverware caddies used to be common accessories on the prairie years ago, when large family gatherings were regular occurrences. A caddy eliminated lugging handfuls of silverware to and from the table, made setting the table a speedy chore and kept utensils ready at attention for the next meal. Our silverware caddy is crafted from traditional, sturdy oak and features a decorative cloverleaf carrying grip. The rounded handle and divider interlock, creating four sections to keep knives, spoons and dinner and salad forks separate and upright for easy identification. Perfect for displaying your good silver, this is an easy afternoon project that will give long-lasting "service" to any dinner table.

OVERALL SIZE:
12½" HIGH
7" WIDE
7" LONG

3" radius

D   D

D   D

A

½" radius

B

D   D

C

D   D

½" squares

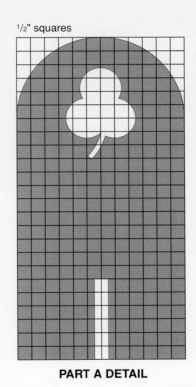

PART A DETAIL

Cutting List				
Key	**Part**	**Dimension**	**Pcs.**	**Material**
A	Handle	½ × 6 × 12"	1	Oak
B	Divider	½ × 6 × 6"	1	Oak
C	Base	½ × 6 × 6"	1	Oak
D	Side	½ × 2 × 6½"	8	Oak

Materials: Wood glue, 16-ga. 1" finish nails, finishing materials.

Note: Measurements reflect the actual thickness of dimensional lumber.

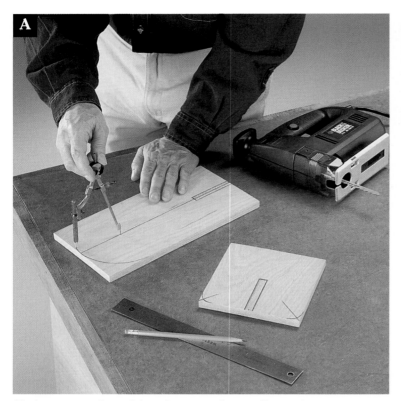

Mark curves and notch locations on reference lines using a compass.

Clamp pieces to your worksurface to ensure steady cuts.

Directions: Silverware Caddy

MAKE THE HANDLE AND DI-VIDER. Corners on the handle and divider are curved, and the pieces are notched to fit together. Start by cutting the handle (A) and divider (B) to size. Mark a centerline down the length of each piece, and draw a ½ × 3" notch at one end centered along each line. At the other end of the handle, place a compass point on the centerline, 3" from the edge, and draw a 3"-rad. curve. At the notched end of the divider, bisect each corner with a 45° line. Place a compass point on the 45° line ¹¹/₁₆" from the corner, and draw ½"-rad. curves on each corner **(photo A).** Clamp each piece to your worksurface, and cut the curves and

notches with a jig saw **(photo B).** Slide the notched ends together to test-fit, and use a chisel to clean out the notches and make adjustments.

CUT THE HANDHOLD. A decorative cloverleaf cutout provides a handhold for the silverware caddy. Transfer the clover template (see *Diagram*) to paper, and trace the pattern onto the handle surface, using the centerline for correct alignment. Cut out each "leaf" of the clover with a 1½"-dia. hole saw **(photo C).** Keep a scrap piece of wood underneath to prevent the hole saw tearing through the other side of the handle. Cut out the clover stem with a

jig saw and chisel. Sand all cuts to remove splinters, and sand the inside of the clover smooth with a 1"-dia. or smaller drum sander attached to your drill **(photo D).**

ASSEMBLE THE BASE AND SIDES. The handle and divider fit together into a base assembly. Cut the sides (D) and base (C) to size, and sand smooth. To make the side frames square, each side end should butt against the face of another side (see *Diagram*). Drill pilot holes at the side joints to ease assembly. Glue and nail four sides together with finish nails and repeat to make two square frames. Check for square when

TIP

When predrilling and nailing the frames of the silverware caddy, angle, or "toenail" each pair of nails toward the middle to provide a stronger joint.

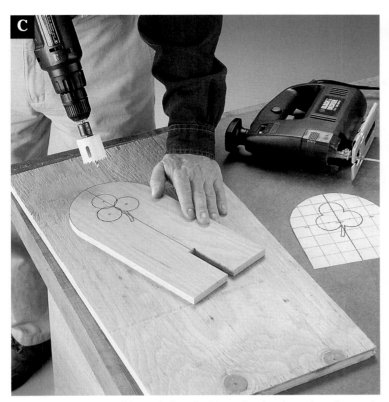

A hole saw cuts quickly and cleanly. Use a backer board underneath to prevent tearouts on the other side of handle.

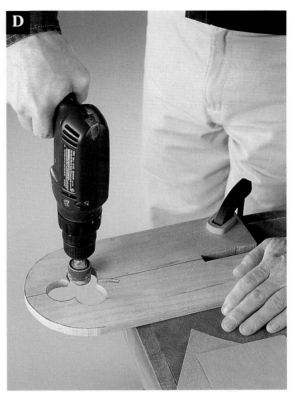

Use a drum sander, or sandpaper wrapped around a dowel, to smooth the inside of the cutout.

nailing, then recess all nail heads with a nail set. Place the base inside one of the frames, drill pilot holes and attach the base with glue and nails. Set the handle and divider inside to test-fit, then apply glue to the joint. Attach the handle and divider to the base assembly with glue and finish nails. Slide the remaining frame over the handle and divider. Keep a 1¼" gap between frames, and attach the frame to the handle and divider with glue and finish nails **(photo E).**

APPLY FINISHING TOUCHES. Fill all nail holes with wood putty. Sand smooth, and apply the finish of your choice. We used a light cherry stain. If you choose paint, use a nontoxic interior-rated latex enamel.

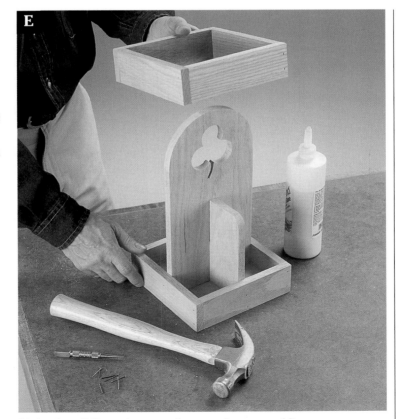

Maintain a 1¼" gap between frames when assembling.

Spice Holder

A light, open design keeps all your spices in plain sight and within easy reach.

PROJECT
POWER TOOLS

So often, spices for your favorite dishes are hidden away in the back corners of kitchen cabinets—used, and then stuffed behind other cooking supplies without a moment's thought. Until, that is, the next time you are fumbling in a dark cabinet for the oregano while a recipe burns on the stove. Experienced chefs always have a spice holder at arm's length. Ours has four shelves, with space for a variety of ingredients. You can take an instant inventory of your supplies and have favorite herbs handy for sudden culinary inspirations.

The series of arcs cut into the spice holder form a gentle wave that gives the pine construction a soft, flowing appeal, and a small scallop in the back echoes this pattern. The fronts of each shelf are rounded, so you can reach for spices without worrying about sharp edges. Though it's designed to rest on a countertop, this spice holder can also be fitted with an additional shelf and mounted on the wall.

CONSTRUCTION MATERIALS

Quantity	Lumber
1	1 × 6" × 8' pine
1	1 × 10" × 8' pine

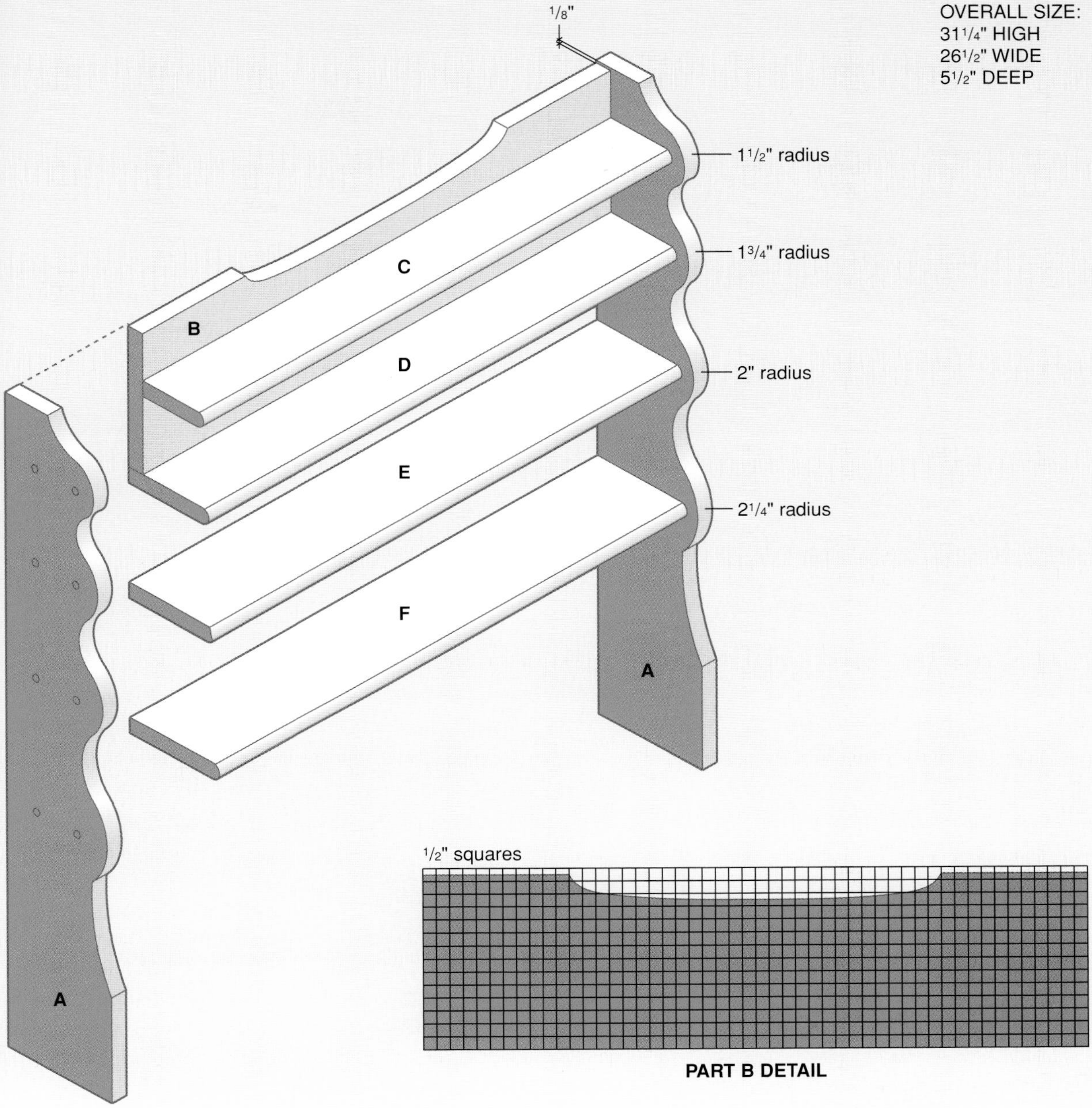
1/8"
OVERALL SIZE:
31 1/4" HIGH
26 1/2" WIDE
5 1/2" DEEP
1 1/2" radius
1 3/4" radius
2" radius
2 1/4" radius
A
B
C
D
E
F
A
1/2" squares

PART B DETAIL

Cutting List

Key	Part	Dimension	Pcs.	Material
A	Side	¾ × 5½ × 31¼"	2	Pine
B	Back	¾ × 6¾ × 25"	1	Pine
C	Shelf	¾ × 3¼ × 25"	1	Pine
D	Shelf	¾ × 4¼ × 25"	1	Pine
E	Shelf	¾ × 4½ × 25"	1	Pine
F	Shelf	¾ × 4¾ × 25"	1	Pine

Materials: Wood glue, #8 screws (1⅝"), ⅜" birch plugs, finishing materials.

Note: Measurements reflect the actual thickness of dimensional lumber.

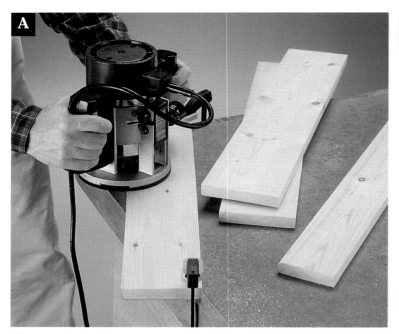

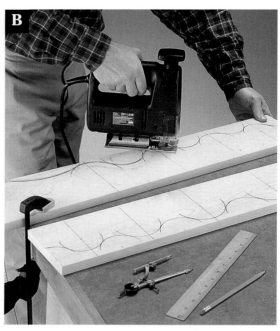

Clamp each shelf to your worksurface for smooth, even router cuts. Flip the shelves to complete each roundover.

Make the side curves with a jig saw. Use clamps to keep parts steady while cutting.

Directions: Spice Holder

MAKE THE SHELVES. The shelves all differ in depth and are cut from dimension lumber. Measure and rip shelves C, D, and E from 1 × 10 pine, and shelf F from 1 × 6 pine, using your circular saw. Clamp each shelf to your worksurface, and round over the front edges of each shelf using a router with a ⅜" roundover bit and bearing guide **(photo A).** Sand all edges smooth.

MAKE THE SIDES. A series of arcs and reference lines indicate cutting lines and shelf positions. Cut the sides (A) to size from 1 × 6 pine, and sand all cuts smooth. Draw reference lines across the sides for the curves and shelves, starting from the bottom of each side, at points 12", 18½", 24", and 28½" along a long edge. The arcs you draw from the template (see *Detail*, page 121) will be centered on these lines. Transfer the template arcs to each side, and blend all of the arcs together with graceful curves. Clamp each side to your worksurface, and use a jig saw to cut along the arcs **(photo B).**

MAKE THE BACK ASSEMBLY. The back is shaped, then attached to two shelves, providing a framework for the spice rack. Cut the back (B) to size from 1 × 10 stock. Draw a curve 1" deep and 14" long, centered

A drum sander makes sanding curves quick and easy.

TIPS

If you do not own a router, you can complete the roundovers on the front edges of each shelf by planing down the edges with a block plane. You will probably find that planing goes more smoothly, if you plane so the wood grain runs "uphill" ahead of the plane. Don't try to remove too much wood at one time; smooth, easy strokes will achieve the best results. Use an orbital sander to smooth the plane cuts and achieve the proper roundover.

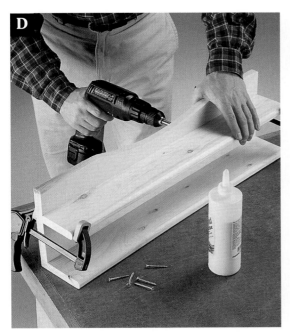

Attach the top shelf to the back assembly from behind with glue and countersunk screws.

Be sure to counterbore all the pilot holes on the sides before driving screws.

on one long edge of the back (see *Diagram,* page 119), and cut with a jig saw. Attach a 1"-dia. drum sander to your drill, and sand the curves of each piece smooth **(photo C).**

Clamp the bottom edge of the back against shelf D, keeping the back flush with the square edge of the shelf. Attach with glue and countersunk 1⅝" screws driven through the bottom of the shelf and into the edge of the back.

When dry, align the top shelf C on the back so the top edge is 2¼" down from the top edge of the back. Glue and clamp in place, and secure with countersunk screws driven through the back and into the shelf **(photo D).**

ATTACH THE REMAINING PARTS. Place the back assembly and remaining shelves in position between the sides. Center the shelves on the reference lines and keep the back edges flush. Use pipe clamps to hold the spice rack together, and counterbore ⅜" pilot holes through the sides and into the ends of each shelf. Keep the counterbores lined up horizontally for an even look. Remove the clamps, apply glue, and then reclamp, continually checking to make sure the assembly is square. Secure the shelves with 1⅝" screws driven through the counterbored pilot holes **(photo E).**

APPLY FINISHING TOUCHES. Insert glued birch button plugs into each counterbored hole and let dry. Finish-sand the entire project, and apply a light oil or stain, and a polyurethane topcoat.

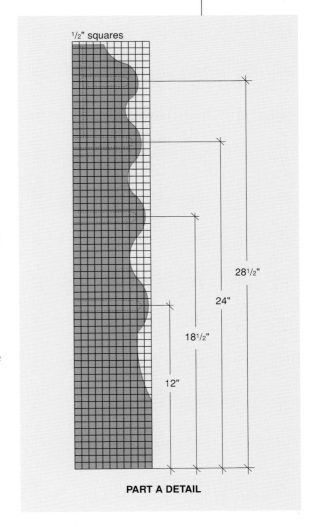

½" squares

28½"

24"

18½"

12"

PART A DETAIL

Changing Screen

When your guests arrive and the house gets crowded, set up this changing screen to create privacy on demand.

CONSTRUCTION MATERIALS

Quantity	Lumber
6	1 × 4" × 8' pine
1	1 × 6" × 6' pine
6	½ × 1⅜" × 8' cap molding
6	¼ × ¼" × 8' quarter-round
1	⅛" × 4 × 8' hardboard

Vacation homes are popular gathering spots for friends and relatives. As a result, space can get pretty tight and privacy becomes a valued commodity. This changing screen helps to remedy the situation by providing what amounts to a portable wall. This three-panel changing screen can be set up in any room, adding a much-needed privacy area. With its attractive wallpapered panels, it can even be used as a room divider to create an intimate space within a larger room.

Because the ⅛"-thick hardboard panels are held in place by common trim moldings, not rabbet grooves, building this changing screen is very simple.

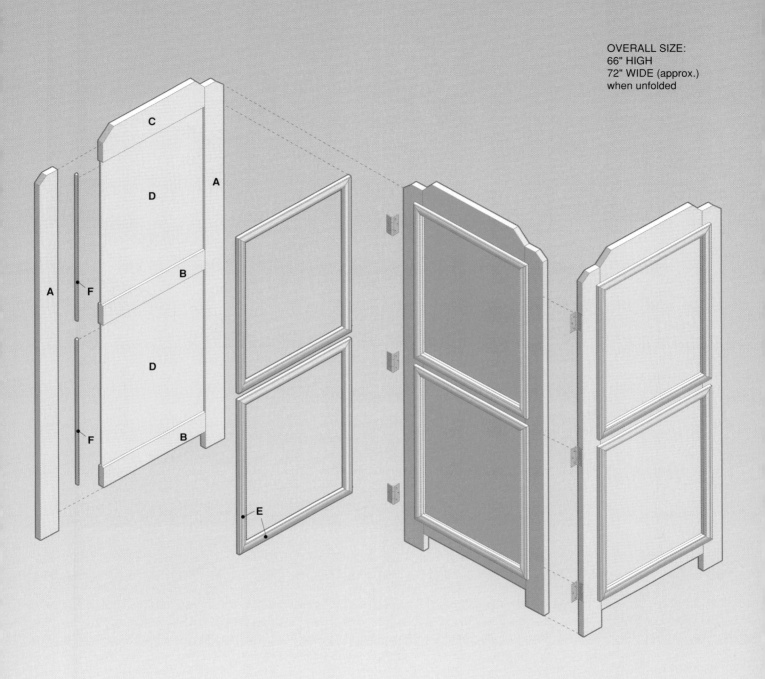

OVERALL SIZE:
66" HIGH
72" WIDE (approx.)
when unfolded

	Cutting List (for three panels)			
Key	**Part**	**Dimension**	**Pcs.**	**Material**
A	Upright	¾ × 3½ × 64"	6	Pine
B	Lower rail	¾ × 3½ × 20"	6	Pine
C	Top rail	¾ × 5½ × 20"	3	Pine

	Cutting List			
Key	**Part**	**Dimension**	**Pcs.**	**Material**
D	Panel	⅛ × 20 × 25¼"	6	Hardboard
E	Front molding	½ × 1⅛ × *	24	Cap molding
F	Rear molding	¼ × ¼ × *	24	Quarter-round

Materials: Glue, 6d finish nails, 1" wire brads, 1½ × 2" brass butt hinges (6), wallpaper (36' of 3'-wide), finishing materials.

Note: Measurements reflect the actual thickness of dimensional lumber.
  *Cut to fit

Clamp the uprights together with their ends flush, and mark the positions for the frame rails.

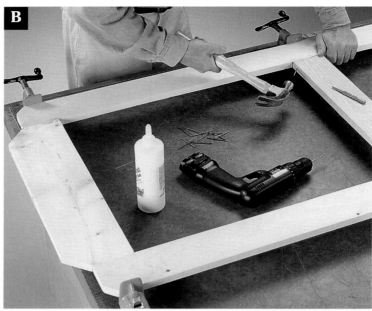

With the rails glued and clamped in place, toenail 6d finish nails through the rails and into the uprights.

Directions: Changing Screen

MAKE THE UPRIGHTS. Each of the three screen panels on the changing screen project is composed of a pine frame with two hardboard panel inserts. The panels are hinged together to create a structure that is self-standing when unfolded. Start by cutting the frame uprights (A) to length from 1 × 4 pine. To help ensure that the frames are uniform, clamp all six uprights together on edge, making sure their ends are flush and square. Designate one end as the bottom, and use a square to mark reference lines across the edges of the uprights, 3" and 31¾" up from the bottom ends, and 3½" down from the top ends **(photo A).** These reference lines mark the position of the bottom edges of the rails. A triangle with 1" legs is trimmed from the top, outside corner of each upright. To draw cutting lines for this triangle, mark a

point on the long edge opposite the reference line, 1" down from the top corner. Mark another point on each top edge, 1" in from the same corner. Using a straightedge, draw a cutting line connecting the two points. Cut along the line with a jig saw or a circular saw. Sand the uprights to smooth out any sharp edges.

MAKE THE RAILS. Cut the lower rails (B) from 1 × 4 and the top rails (C) from 1 × 6. The two top corners of each top rail feature triangular trim cuts similar to those in the tops of the uprights. Simply mark triangular cutoffs with 2" legs at both ends of each top rail (make sure the cuts are on the same edge), and cut with a jig saw or circular saw.

MAKE THE SCREEN FRAMES. The screen panels are built in much the same way as picture frames: simply position the rails between the uprights (using the reference lines drawn on the edges of the uprights), and

glue and clamp the frame so the corners are square. Assemble the three screen panel frames one at a time. First, set a pair of uprights on a level worksurface, so the trimmed corners are facing outward. Position two lower rails and an upper rail against the reference lines on the uprights so the bottom edges of the rails are flush with the lines. (The top rail will extend past the tops of the uprights at the points where the trim cuts start.) Apply glue to the ends of the rails, and pin the rails between the uprights, using pipe clamps to hold the parts in place. With a square, check to make sure the frame is square, and adjust it if needed. After the glue sets, drill pilot holes for 6d finish nails through the rails and into the uprights, and toenail the rails to the uprights **(photo B).** Set all the nail heads with a nail set, and repeat the assembly process to build the two remaining frames.

ADD THE MOLDING FRAMES. Each frame opening is framed in front with cap molding to create surfaces for mounting the panels inside the frames. Cap molding is contoured molding with a built-in recess, usually used on top of base molding. Cut the front molding (E) pieces to fit around each opening, mitering the corners with a power miter saw or back saw and miter box. Attach the cap molding frame pieces around the openings with glue and 1" wire brads driven through pilot holes. Sand all joints and edges smooth. Then, cut the rear molding (F) strips from quarter-round molding so they fit inside the backs of the frame openings. Do not install the rear molding until after the panels are inserted in the opening. Now, fill all nail holes with wood putty, and finish-sand the wood surfaces. Apply your finish of choice—we used primer and enamel latex paint. Be sure to paint the unattached rear molding pieces as well.

MAKE & INSTALL THE SCREEN PANELS. We chose to cover the ⅛"-thick hardboard screen panels with wallpaper before installing them in the frames. You can paint the panels if you prefer—we recommend that you use a paint color that is different from the frame color for a more dramatic effect. If you are applying wallpaper, it's important that you paper both faces of each panel at about the same time to prevent the panels from warping. Start by cutting the panels (D) to size from ⅛"-thick hardboard. Test-fit the panels in each frame to make sure they fit snugly, and trim them if needed. Apply wallpaper or paint to each panel.

Use frames made from quarter-round molding to hold the covered panels against the backs of the molding frames at the front of each opening.

Join the finished panels together with butt hinges, making sure the barrels of the hinges at each joint face in opposite directions.

When the panels are dry, insert them into the frames, up against the back edges of the front molding frames. Install the rear molding frame pieces in frames behind the panels to secure them into the frame openings. Use glue and 6d finish nails to attach the rear molding, being careful not to drip glue on the finished surfaces of the frame panels **(photo C).**

JOIN THE PANELS. The three panels are joined together with 1½ × 2" brass butt hinges so the changing screen will be self-standing when unfolded, and the individual panels can be folded flat against one another for storage. With the panels standing upright, install three hinges at each joint, making sure the barrels of the hinges face in opposite directions on the two joints **(photo D).**

Card Table

*This stylish table proves that card tables don't always
have to be flimsy and unappealing.*

CONSTRUCTION MATERIALS

Quantity	Lumber
1	½" × 4 × 4' oak plywood
2	2 × 2" × 8' pine
2	1 × 3" × 8' pine
3	¾ × ¾" × 8' oak edge molding

The card table has always been thought of as overflow seating for those houseguests who are most lacking in seniority. But the diners assigned to this contemporary wood card table will feel more like they have favored status. The warm tones of the oak tabletop contrast vividly with the painted legs and apron for a lovely effect that will blend into just about any setting— from formal dining to a Friday night poker game.

The fold-up legs on this card table are attached with special fasteners designed just for card tables. You can find these fasteners, as well as the oak apron trim, at most hardware stores or woodworker's shops.

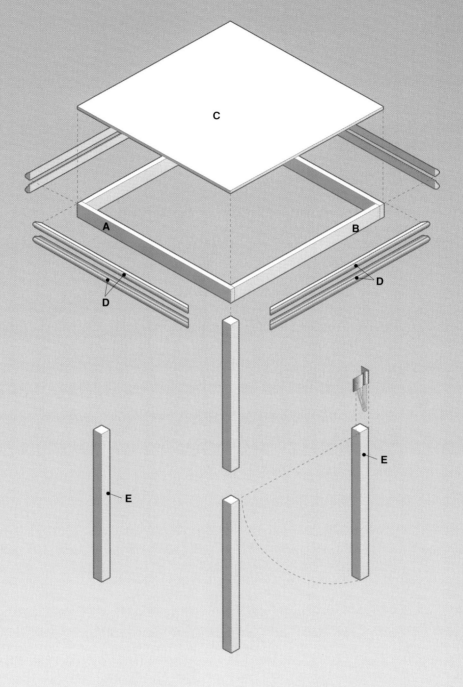

OVERALL SIZE:
29" HIGH
33¼" WIDE
33¼" DEEP

C

A

B

D

D

E

E

Cutting List				
Key	**Part**	**Dimension**	**Pcs.**	**Material**
A	Side apron	¾ × 2½ × 32"	2	Pine
B	End apron	¾ × 2½ × 30½"	2	Pine
C	Tabletop	½ × 32 × 32"	1	Oak plywood

Cutting List				
Key	**Part**	**Dimension**	**Pcs.**	**Material**
D	Edge trim	¾ × ¾ × 32"	8	Oak molding
E	Leg	1½ × 1½ × 28"	4	Pine

Materials: Wood glue, #6 × 1½" wood screws, 2" machine bolts with locking nuts (4), 3d finish nails, oak-tinted wood putty, card-table leg fasteners (4), finishing materials.

Note: Measurements reflect the actual thickness of dimensional lumber.

Directions: Card Table

BUILD THE TABLETOP. The tabletop for this card table is a sheet of oak plywood framed with an apron made from 1 × 3 pine. Strips of oak molding are attached around the top and bottom of the apron to protect the edges of the apron when the table is being stored, and to add a nice decorative accent. Start by cutting the side aprons (A) and end aprons (B) to length. Fasten the end aprons between the side aprons with glue and countersunk wood screws to form a square frame **(photo A).** Keep the outside edges and surfaces of the aprons flush. Next, cut the tabletop (C) to size from ½"-thick plywood using a circular saw and straightedge cutting guide. Position the plywood tabletop on the frame, keeping the outside edges of the tabletop flush with the outer surfaces of the aprons. Fasten the tabletop to the top of the frame with glue and 3d finish nails **(photo B).**

SHAPE THE LEGS. Cut the legs (E) to length. Lay out ¾"-radius curves on each leg end using a compass, and cut the curves with a jig saw to form the roundovers. These allow the legs to pivot smoothly inside the card-table leg fasteners.

Fasten the end aprons between the side aprons with glue and countersunk wood screws to construct the apron frame.

PAINT THE FRAME & LEGS. If you plan to apply a combination finish, as we did, you'll find it easier and neater to paint the legs and frame before you assemble the table and attach the apron trim. Sand the pine surfaces to be painted with medium-grit sandpaper. Wipe the surfaces clean, then apply primer to the aprons and legs. Apply several coats of enamel paint in the color of your choice (we chose blue).

ATTACH THE EDGE TRIM. When the paint has dried, attach the edge trim to the tabletop edges and the aprons. We used plain oak shelf-edge molding, but you may wish to use a more decorative molding type (but be sure to use oak to match the tabletop). Start by cutting the edge trim pieces (D) to length. You'll need to cut a 45° miter at each end of each trim piece, using a power miter saw or hand miter box. The best method is to cut a miter on one end of the first

piece, and position the trim against the apron or tabletop edges. Mark the appropriate length on the uncut end of the trim, cut the 45° miter, and then fasten the edge trim to the aprons or the tabletop edge using wood glue and 3d finish nails. Drill pilot holes through the trim pieces before driving the nails—because it is so hard, oak is prone to splitting. Continue this process, keeping the mitered ends tight when marking for length, until all edge trim has been attached to the aprons and tabletop edges **(photo C).** Be sure to keep the tops of the upper trim pieces flush with the surface of the tabletop. Keep the bottoms of the lower trim pieces flush with the bottoms of the aprons.

FASTEN THE LEGS & HARDWARE. The legs are attached to the table with locking card-table leg fasteners. First, attach a card-table leg fastener to the

Fasten the oak plywood tabletop to the top of the apron frame with glue and finish nails. Oak trim is used to cover the plywood edges.

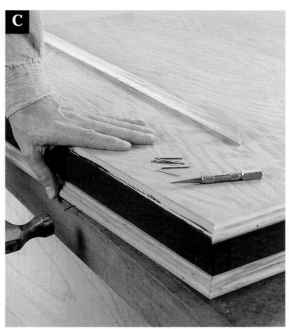

The oak trim fastened at the top and bottom of the apron provides protection and a decorative accent.

Attach the card-table leg fasteners to the rounded ends of the legs, then attach them at the inside corners of the tabletop frame.

apron at each corner of the tabletop frame **(photo D).** Test the legs to make sure they fit properly when folded up, and that the fasteners operate smoothly. Also check to make sure the table is level and stable when resting on a flat surface. Make any needed adjustments to the positioning or length of the legs, then fully tighten all screws.

APPLY FINISHING TOUCHES. Set all finish-nail heads in the table surface, and cover the heads with oak-tinted wood putty. Sand the putty smooth, then sand the unfinished surfaces with medium sandpaper. Finish-sand with fine sandpaper. Wipe the surfaces, then apply sanding sealer for an even finish. Apply wood stain to color the wood (if you are using medium to dark stain, mask the painted surfaces first). Apply two or three light coats of water-based polyurethane to the entire table.

rounded end of each leg by drilling a ¼"-dia. hole through the leg, then securing the fastener to the leg with a 2" machine bolt and locking nut (the fastening method may vary, depending on the brand of hardware you purchase; be sure to read any manufacturer's direc

tions that come with the hardware). Attach the fasteners to the legs with the screws provided with the hardware. Do not tighten the screws completely yet. Next, lay the tabletop upside down on a flat worksurface. Attach the leg fasteners to the insides of the

Sewing Chest

Soft lines, a spacious interior and a removable tray make this chest a perfect companion for sewing, knitting or needlepoint hobbyists.

CONSTRUCTION MATERIALS

Quantity	Lumber
1	¾" × 4' × 8' plywood
1	¼" × 4' × 4' plywood
1	½ × 2¼" × 8' beaded molding

With this clever sewing chest, you can move from room to room in pursuit of your crafting hobby, without leaving a trail of tools and materials in your wake. The padded lid flips up for access to a removable tray and the generous storage compartment below. The up-holstered top can be used as a footrest, a seat, or even a temporary pincushion—just be careful not to mix the uses. This sewing chest is designed to be the perfect size for most sewing, knitting and fabric art projects. It's big enough to hold all your tools and supplies, but still lightweight and portable.

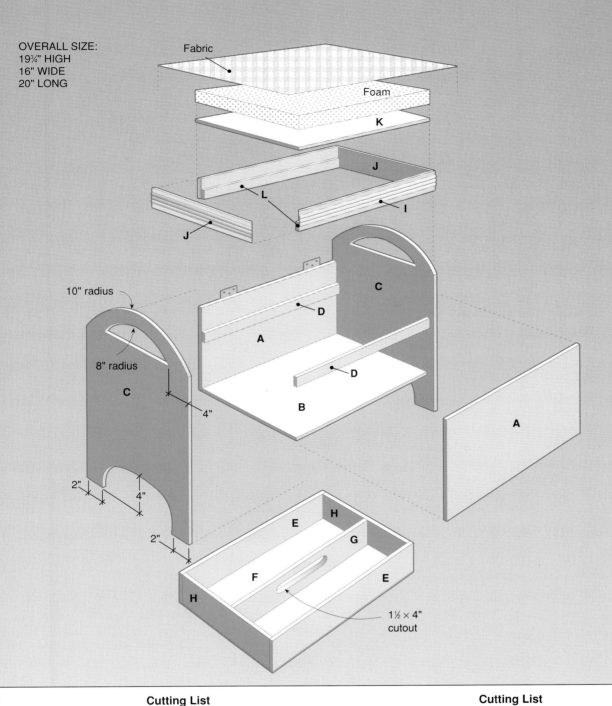

OVERALL SIZE:
19¾" HIGH
16" WIDE
20" LONG

Fabric

Foam

K

J

L

I

J

10" radius

8" radius

C

C

4"

C

D

A

D

B

2"

4"

2"

A

E

H

G

F

H

E

1½ × 4"
cutout

Key	Part	Dimension	Pcs.	Material
A	Front/back	¾ × 9¾ × 18½"	2	Plywood
B	Bottom	¾ × 14 × 18½"	1	Plywood
C	Chest end	¾ × 16 × 20"	2	Plywood
D	Tray cleat	¾ × 1½ × 18¼"	2	Plywood
E	Tray side	¾ × 3 × 18"	2	Plywood
F	Tray bottom	¼ × 13¾ × 18"	1	Plywood

Cutting List

Key	Part	Dimension	Pcs.	Material
G	Tray divider	¾ × 3 × 16½"	1	Plywood
H	Tray end	¾ × 3 × 12¼"	2	Plywood
I	Side molding	½ × 2¼ × 18¼"	2	Molding
J	End molding	½ × 2¼ × 15½"	2	Molding
K	Seatboard	¾ × 14⅜ × 17⅛"	1	Plywood
L	Seat cleat	¾ × 1 × 17¼"	2	Plywood

Cutting List

Materials: Glue, wood screws (#6 × 1¼", #6 × 2"), 4d finish nails, 1" wire brads, 1"-thick foam, upholstery fabric, 1½ × 1¼" butt hinges, finishing materials.

Specialty Items: 1½"-dia. hole saw, scissors.

Note: Measurements reflect the actual size of dimensional lumber.

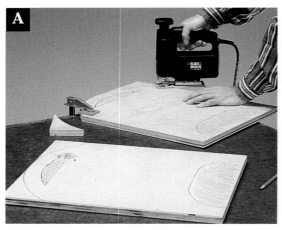

Make the handle cutout and the curves at the top and bottom of the end panels with a jig saw.

Make the ends of the handle cutout in the divider with a hole saw, then connect with a jig saw.

Directions: Sewing Chest

CUT THE CHEST ENDS. The ends of the sewing chest have curved tops and bottoms, and handle cutouts that are made with a jig saw. Start by cutting the ends (C) to size from ¾"-thick plywood. Use a straight-edge to draw a centerline from top to bottom on each side (to use as a reference for drawing the curved cutting lines). To draw cutting lines for the top curves, tack a finishing nail into each end panel, 10" down from the top on the centerline. Tie a string to the nail, and measure out 10" on the string. Tie a pencil at this point. With the string taut, draw a curve from side to side of the end panel. To draw cutting lines for the handle cutouts, adjust the pencil so it is 8" from the nail, and draw a semicircle below the top cutting arc. Connect the points where the 10" curve meets the sides of each end panel to create the straight bottom of the handle cutouts. To make the bottom cutting lines, mark points 2" in from each side of each end panel, at the bottoms. Mark another point 4" up from the bottom of each panel, on

the centerline. Draw an 8"-long line at the 4" mark, parallel to the bottom of each end panel. Connect the end-points of these lines with a smooth arc to the 2" points. Cut the top and bottom curves with a jig saw **(photo A),** and sand smooth with a drum sander attachment on your power drill. Drill starter holes, then make the handle cutouts with a jig saw. Sand the handle cutouts smooth with a thin metal sanding block.

ASSEMBLE THE CHEST. Cut the front and back panels (A), the bottom (B), and the tray cleats (D). Attach the cleats to the inside faces of the front and back panels so the tops of the cleats are 6½" above the bottoms of the panels. Use glue and #6 × 1¼" wood screws. Attach the bottom between the front and back panels with glue

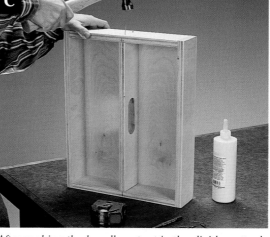

After making the handle cutout in the divider, attach it between the tray ends with glue and finish nails.

and #6 × 2" screws, making sure the ends of the pieces are flush. Install the assembly between the end panels: the underside of the bottom should be flush with the tops of the cutouts on the bottoms of the end panels, and the front and back should each be recessed ¼" from the sides of the end panels. Use glue and #6 × 2" counterbored screws driven through the outside faces of the end panels and into the front, back and bottom. Cut the tray sides (E), tray bottom (F), tray divider (G), and tray ends (H). Mark a centerpoint on one face

After stapling or tacking the upholstery material over the foam-rubber padding, trim off the excess material with scissors.

Sandwich knitting needles or other light items between strips of Velcro® attached to the underside of the seat. Cover the backs of the outer strips with upholstery for a decorative look.

of the divider. Draw a 4"-long line through the centerpoint, parallel to the top and bottom of the divider. Mark points on the line 1¼" on each side of the centerpoint. Install a 1½"-dia. hole saw on your portable drill and drill holes at these points. Connect the holes with a jig saw, then sand smooth with a drum sander attachment to create the handle cutout in the divider **(photo B).** Fasten the tray sides to the tray ends with glue and 4d finish nails. Attach the tray bottom in the same way. Attach the divider between the ends **(photo C).** Use a nail set to set all exposed nail heads.

BUILD THE SEAT. The sewing chest seat is composed of pieces of 2¼"-wide beaded molding that frame a plywood seatboard. The seatboard is padded with 1"-thick foam rubber and covered with upholstery material. Start by cutting the beaded molding to make the sides and ends (I, J) of the seat frame. Use a power miter box or a hand miter box and backsaw to cut 45° miters at

the ends of each frame piece so the pieces fit together to form a square frame. Assemble the frame using glue and 1" wire brads driven through pilot holes at each joint. If you own a picture frame clamp, this is an excellent time to use it. Otherwise, clamp the frame from both directions with bar or pipe clamps, checking to make sure the corners are square. Cut the seat cleats (L) and seatboard (K) to size. Attach the cleats to the sides of the seat frame (after the glue has dried), flush with the bottom edges, using glue and 4d finish nails. Fill plywood edges with putty, finish-sand, and paint the chest before proceeding.

MAKE THE SEAT CUSHION. Cut a piece of 1"-thick foam rubber the same size as the seatboard. Cut a piece of upholstery material large enough to cover the foam and the seatboard, overhanging by at least 4" on each side. Fold the upholstery over the foam and seat board, and tack or staple it along the edges **(photo D).** Set the seat onto the seat cleats in the seat frame, and attach by

driving 4d finish nails through the frame and into the seat board. For a handy touch, cut self-adhesive Velcro® strips and stick them to the underside of the seat. Stick a piece of upholstery fabric to the matching part of each strip **(photo E).** Use the strips to secure knitting needles or other light crafting items. Finally, attach the seat to the chest with 1½ × 1¼" butt hinges **(photo F).**

Attach the seat to the back of the chest with two evenly spaced 1½ × 1¼" butt hinges.

Yard & Garden Cart

With a 4 cu. ft. bin and a built-in rack for long-handled tools, this sleek yard-and-garden cart is hardworking and versatile.

CONSTRUCTION MATERIALS

Quantity	Lumber
1	2 × 6" × 8' cedar
5	2 × 4" × 8' cedar
2	1 × 6" × 8' cedar
2	1 × 4" × 8' cedar
1	1"-dia. × 3' dowel

This sturdy yard-and-garden cart picks up where a plain wheelbarrow leaves off. It includes many clever features to make doing yard work more efficient, without sacrificing hauling space in the bin area.

The notches in the handle frame do double duty as a rack that keeps long-handled tools stable as you rumble across the yard. The handle itself folds down and locks in place like a kickstand when the cart is parked, then flips up to form an extra-long handle that takes advantage of simple physics to make the cart easier to push and steer. And because it's made of wood, this cart will never become rusty or full of dents.

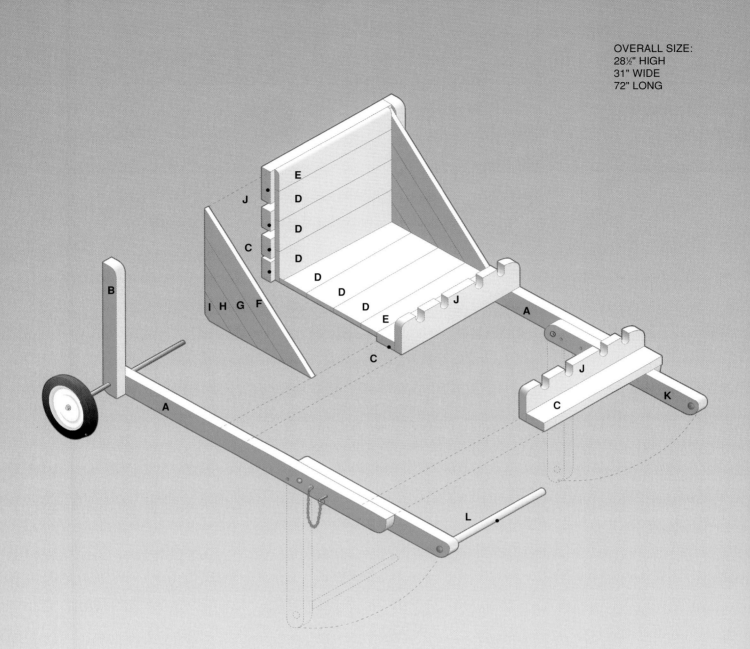

OVERALL SIZE:
28½" HIGH
31" WIDE
72" LONG

Cutting List

Key	Part	Dimension	Pcs.	Material
A	Back support	1½ × 3½ × 57"	2	Cedar
B	Front support	1½ × 3½ × 23½"	2	Cedar
C	Cross rail	1½ × 3½ × 24"	5	Cedar
D	Bin slat	⅞ × 5½ × 22¼"	6	Cedar
E	End slat	⅞ × 3½ × 22¼"	2	Cedar
F	Bin side	⅞ × 3½ × 28"	2	Cedar

Cutting List

Key	Part	Dimension	Pcs.	Material
G	Bin side	⅞ × 3½ × 21"	2	Cedar
H	Bin side	⅞ × 3½ × 14"	2	Cedar
I	Bin side	⅞ × 3½ × 7"	2	Cedar
J	Top rail	1½ × 5½ × 24"	3	Cedar
K	Arm	1½ × 3½ × 32"	2	Cedar
L	Handle	1"-dia. × 21"	1	Dowel

Materials: Deck screws (2", 2½"), 4d finish nails (2), 10" utility wheels (2), steel axle rod (30"), ³⁄₁₆"-dia. cotter pins, ⅜"-dia. hitch pins and chain (2), ⅜ × 4" carriage bolts (2) with lock nuts and washers (4), finishing materials.

Note: Measurements reflect the actual size of dimensional lumber.

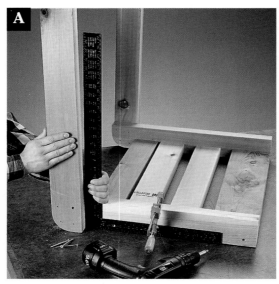

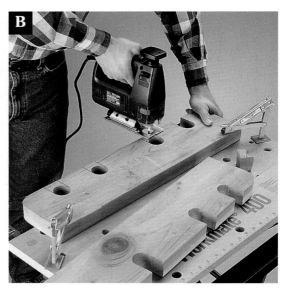

Test with a square to make sure the front supports and back supports are joined at right angles.

Make straight cuts from the edge of each rail to the sides of the holes to make the tool notches.

Directions:
Yard & Garden Cart

BUILD THE CART FRAME. The frame of the cart consists of a pair of L-shaped 2 × 4 assemblies joined together by rails. Start by cutting the back supports (A), front supports (B), three cross rails (C) and one of the top rails (J). Use a compass to draw a curve with a 3½" radius on each end of the back supports and on one end of each front support. When the curves are cut, the ends of these parts will have one rounded corner and one square corner. Cut the curves with a jig saw and sand out any rough spots or saw marks. Position the top rail between the tops of the front supports (the

ends that are square at both corners). Fasten the rail between the supports with glue and 2½"deck screws driven through pilot holes (countersink all pilot holes in this project so the screw heads are recessed). Next, position two cross rails between the front supports, 9" and 14" down from the tops of the front supports. Make sure the cross rails are aligned with the top rail, and attach them with glue and deck screws. Fasten another cross rail between the bottom ends of the front supports; the bottom edge of the cross rail is 3½" up from the bottoms of the front supports and aligned with the other rails. Glue and screw the front supports to the back supports, using a square to make sure the parts are joined at right angles **(photo A).** The unshaped ends of the back supports should be flush with the front and bottom edges of the front supports, and the back supports should be attached to the inside faces of the front supports. Drill cen-

tered, ½"-dia. holes for the wheel axles through the bottoms of the front supports and back supports, 1¾" in from the inside corner where the front and back supports are joined.

CUT THE NOTCHED TOP RAILS. Cut the two remaining top rails (J). These rails contain notches that are aligned to create a rack for tool handles. Before cutting the tool notches into the rails, use a compass to draw 1½"-radius roundover curves at each end along one side of each rail. Cut the roundovers with a jig saw. To make the tool notches in the top rails, first draw a reference line 1½" in from the rail edge between the roundovers. Mark four drilling points on the line, 3¾" and 8¼" in from each end. Use a drill and a spade bit to drill 1½"-dia. holes through the drilling points on each rail. Use a square to draw cutting lines from the sides of the holes to the near edge of each rail. Cut along the lines with a jig saw to complete the tool notches **(photo B).**

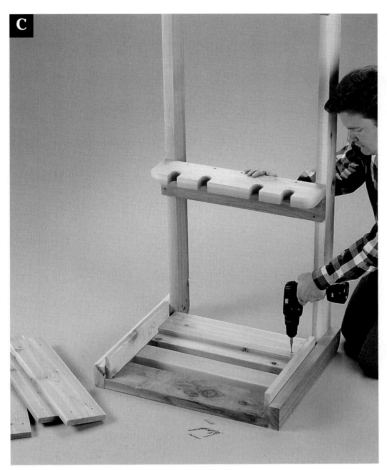

C

Attach the bin slats to the front supports, leaving a ⅞"-wide gap at both ends of each slat.

ATTACH RAILS BETWEEN THE BACK SUPPORTS. Cut two cross rails (C) and lay them flat on your worksurface. Attach a top rail to the edges of each cross rail, so the ends are flush and the edges of the top rails with the tool notches are facing up. Use 2½" deck screws driven at 4" intervals through the top rails and into the edges of the cross rails. Then set one of the assemblies on the free ends of the back supports, flush with the edges. The free edge of the cross rail should be flush with the ends of the back supports. Attach the cross rail with deck screws driven down into the back support. Attach the other

rail assembly to the top edges of the back supports so the top rail faces the other rail assembly, and the free edge of the cross rail is 21" from the front ends of the back supports. This completes the assembly of the cart frame.

ATTACH THE BIN SLATS. The bin portion of the yard-and-garden cart is formed by cedar slats that are attached to the cart frame. Start by cutting the bin slats (D) and end slats (E) to size. Position one end slat and three bin slats between the front supports, with the end slat flush with the edge of the front cross rail and the last bin slat butted against the back supports. There should be a ⅞" gap

between each end of each slat and the front supports. Attach the slats with glue and 2" deck screws driven down through the slats and into the cross rails **(photo C).** Fasten the rest of the bin slats to the top edges of the back supports, with a ⅞" recess at each end. Start with the slat that fits at the bottom of the bin, and work your way up, driving screws down into the tops of the back supports. Fasten the final end slat so it fits between the last bin slat and the lower cross rail on the back supports. Use a grinder or belt sander with a coarse belt to round over the front edges of the front end slat and front supports **(photo D).**

ATTACH THE BIN SIDES. The bin sides fill in the V-shape between the front and back supports. They fit into the recess created between the bin slats and the front supports. First, square-cut the bin sides (F, G, H, I) to the lengths shown in the *Cutting List* on page 135. Then, draw a miter-cutting line at each end of each bin side. Make the miter cuts with a circular saw and straightedge, or with a power miter saw if you have one. Fit the short, V-shaped sides into the openings at the sides of the bin, and attach them to the front supports with 2" deck screws. Install the rest of the bin sides in the correct order **(photo E).**

> **TIP**
>
> *Cut pieces of sheet aluminum or galvanized metal to line the cart bin for easy cleaning after hauling. Simply cut the pieces to fit inside the bin, then attach them with special roofing nails that have rubber gaskets under the nail heads. Make sure that no sharp metal edges are sticking out from the bin.*

Round over the tips of the front supports and the front edge of the end slat, using a belt sander.

Fasten the bin sides in a V-shape with glue and deck screws.

Drill a pilot hole through each arm and into the ends of the handle, then drive a 4d finish nail into the hole to secure the handle.

MAKE THE ARMS. The arms (K) serve a double purpose. First, they support the handles when you wheel the cart. Second, they drop down and lock in place to support the cart in an upright position. Cut the arms (K) to length. Mark the center of each end of each arm, measuring from side to side. Measure down 3½" from each centerpoint, and mark a point. Set the point of a compass at each of these points, and draw a 1¾"-radius semicircle at each end of both arms. Cut the curves with a jig saw. Then drill a 1"-dia. hole for the handle dowel at one of the centerpoints on each arm. At the other centerpoint, drill a ⅜"-dia. guide hole for a carriage bolt.

ATTACH THE ARMS. The arms are attached with carriage bolts to the back supports. Drill ⅜"-dia. holes for carriage bolts through each back support, 19" from the handle end, and centered between the top and bottom edges of the supports. Insert a ⅜"-dia. × 4"-long carriage bolt through the outside of each ⅜"-dia. hole in the back supports. Slip a washer over each bolt, then slip the arms over the carriage bolts. Slip another washer over the end of each bolt, then secure the arms to the supports by tightening a lock nut onto each bolt. Do not overtighten the lock nut—the arms need to be loose enough that they can pivot freely. Cut the handle (L) to length from a 1"-dia. dowel (preferably hardwood). Slide it into the 1"-dia. holes in the ends of the arms. Secure the handle by drilling pilot holes for 4d finish nails through each arm and into the dowel **(photo F),** then driving a finish nail into the dowel at each end.

ATTACH THE WHEELS. The wheels for the cart are 10"-dia. utility wheels fitted over a steel axle rod, and locked in place

Secure the wheels by inserting a cotter pin into a hole at the end of each axle, then bending down the arms of the pin with pliers.

do) into each hole to secure the arms. To prevent losing the pins when you remove them, attach them to the back supports with a chain or a piece of cord. Now, remove the pins and lift the arms up so they are level with the tops of the back supports. Drill ⅜"-dia. holes through the arms and back supports, about 12" behind the first pin holes, for locking the arms in the cart-pushing position.

APPLY FINISHING TOUCHES. Smooth out all the sharp edges on the cart with a sander. Also sand the surfaces slightly. Apply two coats of exterior wood stain to the wood for protection. Squirt some penetrating/ lubricating oil or teflon lubricant onto the axles on each side of each wheel to reduce friction.

with cotter pins. The wheels and steel axle rod can be purchased at a hardware store (make sure to buy an axle rod that fits the holes in the hubs of the wheels). Cut the axle rod to 30" in length with a hacksaw, and deburr it with a file or a bench grinder. (Rough-grit sandpaper will also work, but it takes longer and is hard on the hands.) Secure the axle rod in a vise, or clamp it to your work-surface, and use a steel twist bit to drill a ³⁄₁₆"-dia. hole ⅛" in from each end of the axle. Slip the the axle through the ½"-dia. holes drilled at the joints between the front and back supports, then slide two washers over the ends of the axles. Slip a wheel over each axle, add two washers, then insert a ³⁄₁₆"- dia. cotter pin into each of the holes drilled at the ends of the axle. Secure the wheels by bending down the ends of the cotter pins with a pair of pliers **(photo G).**

LOCK THE ARMS IN PLACE. On a flat surface, fold down the arm/handle assembly so the arms are perpendicular to the ground. Drill a ⅜"-dia. guide hole through each back support, 1" below the carriage bolt that attaches the arms to the supports. Extend the holes all the way through the arms **(photo H).** Insert a ⅜"-dia. hitch pin (or hinge pins will

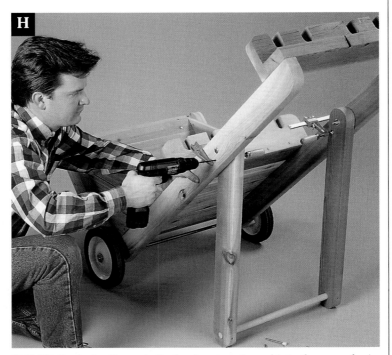

Drill ⅜"-dia. holes through the back supports and into the arms for inserting the hitch pins that lock the arms in position.

Cottage Clock

This cottage clock uses wood appliqués to reproduce an early 19th century clock design.

This reproduction of a "cottage clock" style mantel clock is modeled after a design by Eli Terry from 1816. The mantel clock emerged as a mainstay of the American home back in Colonial times. Although the first models customarily were set on the fireplace mantel, the basic design has evolved to include many types of small clocks that can be positioned anywhere in your home. The primary feature that most mantel clocks share is their size—large enough to be noticed, but smaller than an upright floor clock. Many mantel clocks, including the "cottage clock" design shown here, have a door or false door on the front of the clock cabinet. The doors usually have an upper panel that contains the clock face, and a decorative lower panel (lower panels frequently are made of glass to reveal the pendulum on mechanical clocks).

Making the cabinet for this cottage clock is a simple, inexpensive project that can easily be accomplished in a single afternoon. We used ½"-thick clear pine to build the cabinet frame (most clocks of this type were made with pine, frequently with a hardwood veneer layer). The decorative elements are created with milled moldings and appliqués. The clock itself is an inexpensive battery-operated model. Most woodworker's stores and craft stores carry a wide selection of clocks.

CONSTRUCTION MATERIALS

Quantity	Lumber
1	½ × 6" × 4' pine
1	¾ × 3½" × 4' pine
1	⅛ × ¾" × 5' pine shelf nosing
1	½ × 2¼" × 3' pine casing
1	½ × 1⅛" × 3' cap molding

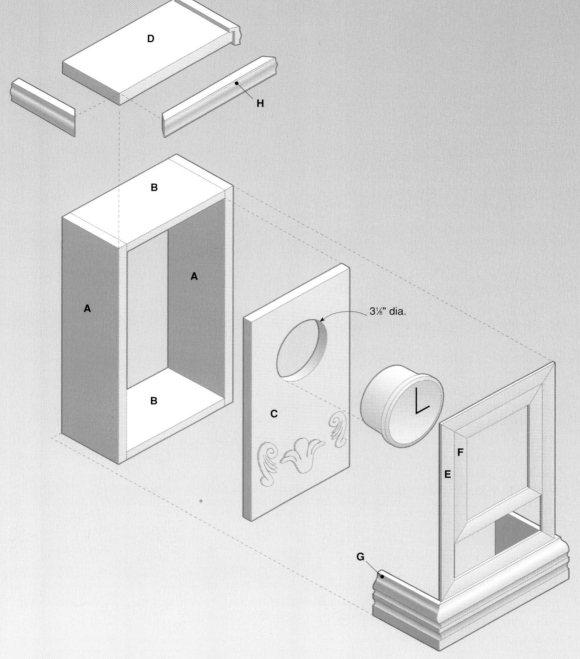

OVERALL SIZE:
13" HIGH
4" DEEP
7¾" WIDE

3⅛" dia.

Cutting List

Key	Part	Dimension	Pcs.	Material
A	Side	½ × 3½ × 12"	2	Pine
B	End	½ × 3½ × 6"	2	Pine
C	Face board	½ × 6 × 11"	1	Pine
D	Crown board	¾ × 3½ × 7"	1	Pine

Cutting List

Key	Part	Dimension	Pcs.	Material
E	Outside trim	⅛ × ¾" × *	4	Shelf nosing
F	Inside trim	⅛ × ¾" × *	4	Shelf nosing
G	Base molding	½ × 2¼" × *	3	Pine casing
H	Crown piece	½ × 1⅛" × *	3	Cap molding

Materials: Glue, 1" wire brads, 3⅛"-dia. battery-powered clock, decorative wood carvings, finishing materials.

Note: Measurements reflect the actual thickness of dimensional lumber.
* Cut to fit

Directions: Cottage Clock

MAKE THE FACE BOARD. This cottage clock cabinet is essentially a pine frame with a cover and a few decorative accents. The battery-operated clock fits into a hole in the front of the cabinet cover—called the face board. Cut the face board (C) to size from ½"-thick pine (most building centers carry ½"-thick solid boards in varying widths and lengths with their shelving and craft products). The size of the cutout for the clock should be based on the diameter of your clock back. The clock we installed has a 3⅛" back diameter. To make the cutout for the clock, add 1½" to the *radius* (½ the diameter) of the clock back, measure down that amount from the top of the face board, and draw a reference line. Next, measure in 3" from one side of the face board and mark a point on the reference line to find the center-point for the cutout. Set a compass to the radius of the clock back (in our case, 1⁹⁄₁₆"). Drill a starter hole inside the circle, and make the cutout with a jig saw. Because the flange of the clock face will cover the edges of the hole, it's okay if the cut is a little rough.

MAKE THE CABINET. The clock cabinet frames the face board. Begin by cutting the sides (A) and ends (B) to

Use the face board as a guide when nailing together the corners of the cabinet frame.

Attach strips of miter-cut cap molding to the front and sides of the crown board, then attach the assembly to the top of the cabinet.

length from 3½"-wide ½"-thick pine. Fasten the sides and ends into a frame, using the face board as a guide. The cabinet sides should overlap the cabinet ends. Make the joints with glue and 1" wire brads, driven through the sides and into the ends. Remove the face board from the frame, and apply glue to the edges. Reinsert it into the frame so the front face is flush

with the front edges of the cabinet frame. Drive a few 1" wire brads through the frame and into the edges of the face board **(photo A).** Although pine is a soft wood, it is a good idea to drill tiny pilot holes for the brads before you drive them. Use a pad sander with fine (about 150-grit) sandpaper to even out all the joints, as

TIP

Decorative wood carvings, sold at most wood-worker's or craft stores, are generally made from oak or birch, but they will blend in with pine, especially if a darker stain is used. When selecting any appliqués (carvings or otherwise), bring a template of the project with you to the store so you can test out different shapes and combinations.

well as smooth out the surfaces of the cabinet.

ATTACH THE CROWN. The crown is the decorative top on the clock cabinet. It is made by framing a piece of ¾"-thick pine with three pieces of ½"-thick × 1⅛"-wide cap molding. Cut the crown board (D) to length, and sand the edges smooth. Then, miter-cut the cap molding into three crown pieces (H) that frame the front and side of the crown board—start by cutting the front strip with 45° ends, then cut the side strips to fit. The back ends of the side strips should be square-cut. Apply glue to the crown pieces, then attach them to the crown board with 1" wire nails. Then, fasten the crown assembly to the top of the cabinet, making sure the back edges are flush and the overhang is equal on both sides, using glue and 1" wire nails (photo B).

ATTACH THE BASE MOLDING. The base molding is made and installed exactly like the pieces of cap molding that frame the crown board. Instead of cap molding, however, use ½ × 2¼" case molding (case molding with decorative contours is a good choice). Cut the base molding pieces (G) to fit around the front and sides of the frame and form clean mitered corners. Attach them, then finish-sand the cabinet.

FRAME THE FACE BOARD. We added decorative trim (⅛ × ¾" shelf nosing) to the clock to create a false door frame that is glued to the face board. A second frame inside the first divides the false door into upper and lower panels. Cut the outside trim pieces (E) to fit around the perimeter of the face board, miter-cutting the

Use ⅛ × ¾" shelf nosing to make frames on the face board, creating the illusion of a cabinet door with upper and lower panels.

For a decorative touch, we glued a set of milled wood carvings (two small seraphs and a tulip design) to the lower panel of the face board.

corners. Using glue only, attach the outside trim (photo C). Then, cut the inside trim (F) to make the internal frame. Check to make sure the clock cutout is centered within the internal frame, then attach the inside trim. Rest a book on the trim frames while the glue dries.

DECORATE THE LOWER PANEL. Glue milled wooden carvings (or add another decorative element, such as stencils) to the lower panel for a nice

decorative touch (photo D).

APPLY FINISHING TOUCHES. Fill any exposed holes with untinted wood putty. Sand the surfaces, and apply your finish of choice (we used walnut stain with a tung-oil topcoat). Install the clock according to the manufacturer's directions. OPTION: If the back of the clock will be visible, cut a back panel to fit inside the frame, using ½"-thick pine. Sand and finish the back of the clock.

Paper Towel Holder

*This sturdy dispenser includes a convenient storage shelf
to keep handy items at close reach.*

CONSTRUCTION MATERIALS

Quantity	Lumber
1	¾ × 11 × 48" MDF
1	1"-dia. × 18" oak dowel
1	½"-dia. × 18" oak dowel

*MDF = medium-density fiberboard

Curved ends soften the profile of this paper towel holder and give you better access to the paper towels. The 2½ × 11 × 11½" compartment shelf is great for keeping boxes of foil, plastic wrap, lunch bags and other frequently used dry goods within easy reach. Replacing the paper towel rolls is a simple matter of withdrawing the 1" oak rod.

Though it is ideally suited for kitchen use, you may want to build several of these heavy-duty units to use in your basement, garage and laundry area. With ¾"-thick sides, shelf and a large 11 ×17½" base, it will stand up to years of use, even when mounted in a high-traffic area. And if left unmounted on a countertop or workbench, this paper towel holder is heavy enough to resist sliding and tipping.

OVERALL SIZE:
9¾" HIGH
17½" WIDE
11" DEEP

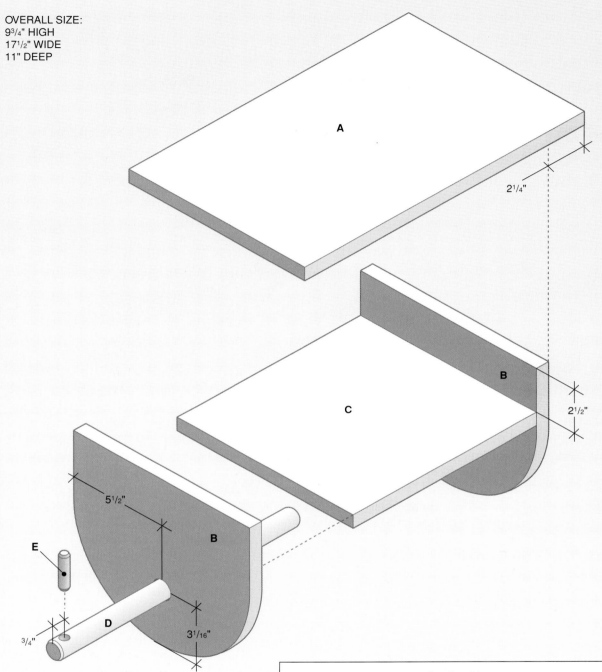

A	
B	
C	
E	
D	

2¼"

2½"

5½"

3¹/₁₆"

¾"

Cutting List				
Key	**Part**	**Dimension**	**Pcs.**	**Material**
A	Top	¾ × 11 × 17½"	1	MDF
B	End	¾ × 11 × 9¼"	2	MDF
C	Shelf	¾ × 11 × 11½"	1	MDF
D	Rod	1"-dia. × 15"	1	Oak dowel
E	Stop dowel	½"-dia. × 2"	1	Oak dowel

Materials: Wood glue, #6 × 1½" screws, 4d finish nails, putty, finishing materials.

Note: Measurements reflect the actual thickness of dimensional lumber.

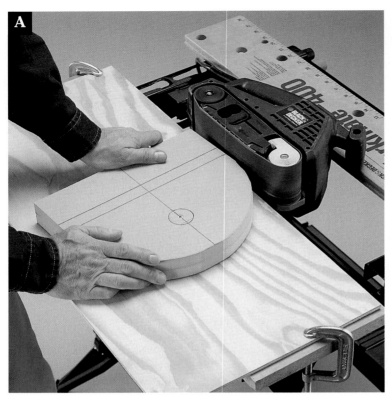

Temporarily screw the two end pieces together through the center-point of the dowel rod hole, and finish the curves with a belt sander.

Drill through ends into scrap plywood to make clean holes and to protect your worksurface.

Directions: Paper Towel Holder

MAKE THE ENDS. Begin by cutting the end blanks (B) to size. On each end, mark the shelf location and the center-point for the rod holes and semicircles (see *Diagram*). Use a compass set to a 3¹⁄₁₆" radius to draw the curves.

To ensure that both end pieces are identical, screw them together at the center-point of the rod hole, then cut both ends at the same time with a jig saw. Belt-sand the two ends smooth while they are still secured together **(photo A).** Unscrew the pieces and drill the rod hole through each end, using a 1⅛"-dia. spade bit **(photo B).**

ASSEMBLE THE SHELF AND TOP. Cut the top (A) and shelf (C) to size, and sand smooth. Drill countersunk pilot holes for attaching the top to the ends. (If you will be mounting the holder to a cabinet, also drill countersunk pilot holes through the bottom face of the top piece, in the areas where the top will overhang the end pieces.) Also drill pilot holes through the ends where the shelf will be attached with finish nails. Join the shelf and ends with glue and 4d finish nails. Attach the top with glue and 1½" wood screws.

CUT THE ROD AND DOWEL. To hold the rod firmly in place while drilling the hole for the stop dowel, build a simple V-jig by using your circular saw to cut a V-shaped notch across the middle of an 18"-long piece of 2 × 8. Set your saw blade at a 45° angle to cut the V-notch **(photo C).**

Cut the oak rod (D) and stop dowel (E) to length. Measure and mark a centerpoint ¾" in from one end of the rod. Clamp the rod onto the V-jig and use a portable drill guide to drill the ½" stop dowel hole through the centerpoint **(photo D).**

TIP:

To drill straight holes into dowels and rods, make sure your portable drill guide rests flat on the 2 × 8 sides of the V-jig. To make your V-jig more stable, mount it onto a larger piece of ¾" plywood.

With your saw set to 1½" depth, make two 45° cuts across the middle of an 18" length of 2 × 8 to create a V-jig.

Clamp rod in V-jig and support portable drill guide on the flat sides of the 2 × 8 to create a straight hole.

Clamp your belt sander on its side on your worksurface, then clamp or nail a scrap piece of wood close to the belt, at an angle of about 45°. Apply a strip of tape ⅛" from each end of the dowel, then rest the dowel against the angled guide and *chamfer* (bevel) each end of the dowel by rotating it against the spinning belt **(photo E).** Also chamfer the stop dowel ends in the same fashion, then glue it into the oak rod.

APPLY FINISHING TOUCHES. Recess all nail heads using a nail set, and fill the holes with putty. Sand the entire unit to 150-grit smoothness, and apply the paint of your choice. If you are mounting the holder underneath a cabinet, attach it with screws driven through the pilot holes in the top.

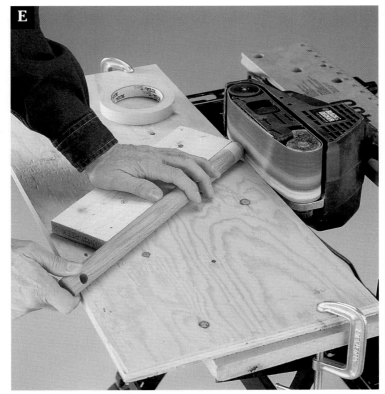

Use a mounted belt sander and an angle guide made from a block of wood screwed to a plywood base to create precise chamfers.

Cabin Marker

Hidden driveways and remote roads won't escape first-time visitors if they are marked with a striking, personalized cabin marker.

Trips to a friend's cabin or vacation home, though usually enjoyable, often start on a confusing note. "Do you have the address written down?" is a common refrain when the fourth left turn leads into a gravel road. You can put an end to the last-minute guesswork by displaying your name, address and mailbox at the head of your driveway—saving your friends (and your postal worker) some time. And on a safety note, emergency vehicles are much more apt to spot your home quickly with a well-marked address.

The simple design of the cabin marker is suitable for almost any yard. Its height ensures a certain level of prominence, but the cedar material and basic construction allow it to fit right in with its natural surroundings.

One of the greatest features of the cabin marker is likely to be the least noticed—the base section. The base is a multi-tiered pyramid of 4 × 4 cedar timbers. It provides ample weight and stability, so you will not need to go to the trouble of digging a hole or pouring concrete. Just position the marker wherever you want it, and stake it in place. Much more attractive than a simple mailbox stand, this project will provide just the touch of originality that your cabin or vacation home deserves.

CONSTRUCTION MATERIALS

Quantity	Lumber
1	1 × 6" × 8' cedar
1	2 × 2" × 6' cedar
4	2 × 4" × 8' cedar
3	4 × 4" × 8' cedar

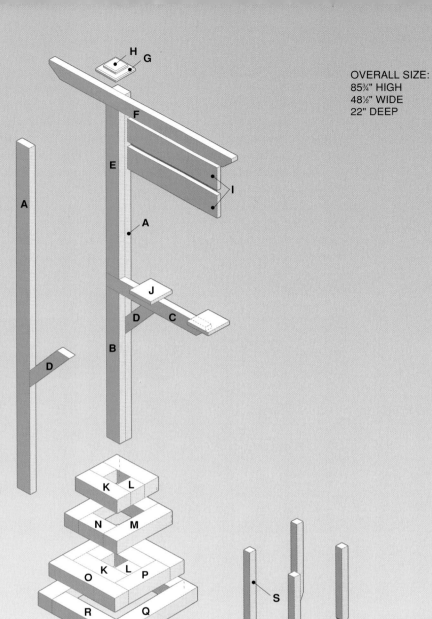

OVERALL SIZE:
85¾" HIGH
48½" WIDE
22" DEEP

Cutting List

Key	Part	Dimension	Pcs.	Material
A	Post side	1½ × 3½ × 84"	2	Cedar
B	Post section	1½ × 3½ × 36½"	1	Cedar
C	Mailbox arm	1½ × 3½ × 23½"	1	Cedar
D	Mailbox brace	1½ × 3½ × 17½"	2	Cedar
E	Post section	1½ × 3½ × 40½"	1	Cedar
F	Sign arm	1½ × 3½ × 48½"	1	Cedar
G	Top plate	⅞ × 5½ × 5½"	1	Cedar
H	Cap	⅞ × 3½ × 3½"	1	Cedar
I	Sign board	⅞ × 5½ × 24"	2	Cedar
J	Mailbox cleat	⅞ × 5½ × 5⅞"	2	Cedar

Cutting List

Key	Part	Dimension	Pcs.	Material
K	Base piece	3½ × 3½ × 10½"	4	Cedar
L	Base piece	3½ × 3½ × 4½"	4	Cedar
M	Base piece	3½ × 3½ × 15"	2	Cedar
N	Base piece	3½ × 3½ × 7"	2	Cedar
O	Base piece	3½ × 3½ × 17½"	2	Cedar
P	Base piece	3½ × 3½ × 11½"	2	Cedar
Q	Base piece	3½ × 3½ × 22"	2	Cedar
R	Base piece	3½ × 3½ × 14"	2	Cedar
S	Stake	1½ × 1½ × 18"	4	Cedar

Materials: Moisture-resistant wood glue, epoxy glue, deck screws (1¼", 2", 2½", 4"), #10 screw eyes (8), S-hooks (4), ⅜"-dia. × 5" galvanized lag screws with 1" washers (4), finishing materials.

Note: Measurements reflect the actual thickness of dimensional lumber.

Directions: Cabin Marker

MAKE THE POST. The post is made in three 2 × 4 layers. Two post sections and two arms form the central layer, which is sandwiched between two full-height post sides. The arms extend out from the post to support a mailbox and an address sign on the finished project. Begin by cutting the mailbox arm (C) and sign arm (F) to length. One end of the mailbox arm and both ends of the sign arm are cut with decorative slants on their bottom edges. To cut the ends of the arms to shape, mark a point on each end, 1" down from a long edge. On the opposite long edge, mark a point 2½" in from the end. Draw a straight line connecting the points, and cut along the line. Cut the post sides (A) and post sections (B, E) to size. To assemble the post, you will sandwich the sections and the arms between the sides. Set one side on a flat worksurface, and position the lower post section (B) on top of it, face to face, with the ends flush. Attach the post section to the side with glue and 2½" deck screws. Position the mailbox arm on the side, making sure the square end is flush with the edge of the side. Check with a square to make sure the mailbox arm is square to the side, and attach the workpieces. Butt the end of the upper post section (E) against the top edge of the mailbox arm, and attach the upper post section **(photo A).** Position the sign arm at the top of the assembly so it extends 30" past the post on the side where the mailbox arm protrudes. Attach the sign arm to the post side with glue and deck screws. Finally, apply glue to the remaining side, and attach it to the post sections with glue and 4" deck screws, making sure all the ends are flush.

ATTACH THE MAILBOX CLEATS & BRACES. The mailbox cleats provide a stable nailing surface for a "rural-style" mailbox on the mailbox arm. The mailbox braces are 2 × 4 workpieces that are fastened to the post

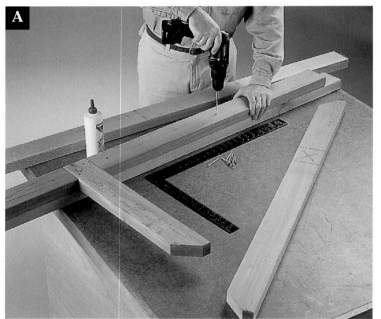

Butt an end of the upper section against the top edge of the mailbox arm, and fasten it to the side.

Position a mailbox brace on each side of the mailbox arm, and fasten them to the post and arm.

Apply glue to the bottom face of the cap, and center it on the top of the post.

and mailbox arm to provide support. Cut the mailbox cleats (J) to size, and sand them to smooth out any rough spots. Center the cleats on the top of the mailbox arm. The front-most cleat should overhang the front of the mailbox arm by 1". Center the remaining cleat 12½" in from the front of the mailbox arm. Attach the cleats with glue and 2½" deck screws. Cut the mailbox braces (D) to length. In order for the mailbox braces to be fastened to the post and mailbox arm, their ends must be cut at an angle. Use a power miter box, or a backsaw and miter box, to miter-cut each end of each mailbox brace at a 45° angle—make sure the cuts slant toward each other (see *Diagram*, page 149). Position a mailbox brace against the side of the mailbox arm so one end is flush with the top edge of the mailbox arm and the other rests squarely against the post. Drill pilot holes, and attach the mailbox braces with glue and 2½" deck screws **(photo B).**

COMPLETE THE POST TOP. The post assembly is capped with a post top and cap made of 1" dimension lumber. Cut the top plate (G) and cap (H) to size. Using a power sander, make ¼"-wide × ¼"-deep bevels along the top edges of the top and cap. Center the top on the post, and attach it with moisture-resistant glue and 2"deck screws, then center the cap on the top, and attach it **(photo C).**

MAKE THE BASE. The base for the cabin marker is a pyramid made from 4 × 4" cedar frames. The frames increase in size from top to bottom and are stacked to create a four-level pyramid effect. A fifth frame

is fitted inside one of the frames to make a stabilizer frame for the bottom of the post. The bottom frame is fastened to stakes driven into the ground to provide a secure anchor that does not require digging holes and pouring concrete footings. Cut the 4 × 4" base pieces for all five frames (K, L, M, N, O, P, Q, R). Assemble them into five frames according to the *Diagram*, page 149. Use 4" deck screws driven into the pilot holes with 1½"-deep counterbores to join the frame pieces. After all five frames are built, join one of the small frames and the two next-smallest frames together in a pyramid, using moisture-resistant glue and 4" deck screws **(photo D).** Invert the pyramid and insert the other small frame into the opening in the third-smallest frame. Secure with deck screws (this inside frame helps stabilize the post end). Set the base assembly on top of the large frame—do not attach them. Insert the post into the opening, and secure it with ⅜"-dia. × 5"-long lag screws, driven through the top frame and into the post. (NOTE: The large frame is anchored to the ground on site before it is attached to the pyramid.)

MAKE THE SIGN BOARDS. Cut the sign boards (I) to size, and sand them to create a smooth surface. We stenciled the address and name onto the signs, but you can use adhesive letters, freehand painting, a router with a veining bit, a woodburner—whichever technique you decide on, test it on a sanded scrap of cedar before working on the signs.

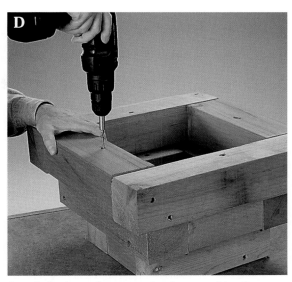

Attach the base tiers to each other, working from top to bottom.

APPLY FINISHING TOUCHES. Join the two signs together with #10 screw eyes and S-hooks. Drill pilot holes for the screw eyes in the sign arm and signs. Apply epoxy glue to the threads of the screws before inserting them. Apply your finish of choice (we used an exterior wood stain), and position the bottom frame of the base in the desired location in your yard. The area should be flat and level so the post is plumb. Check the frame with a level. Add or remove dirt around the base to achieve a level base before installing. Cut the stakes (S) to length, and sharpen one end of each stake. Set the stakes in the inside corners of the frame, then drive them into the ground until the tops are lower than the tops of the frame. Attach the stakes to the frames with deck screws. Center the cabin marker on the bottom frame, and complete the base by driving 5" lag screws through the tops of the base into the bottom frame.

Plant Stand

Wherever you need it, this cedar plant stand provides a setting in which your plants will thrive.

CONSTRUCTION MATERIALS

Quantity	Lumber
1	1 × 8" × 8' cedar
1	1 × 8" × 6' cedar
1	1 × 4" × 4' cedar
1	1 × 2" × 4' cedar
1	1 × 2" × 6' cedar

Though it looks simple, our plant stand is designed to serve many needs. On its tall top shelf, small plants will catch plenty of sunlight. The wide lower shelf, reinforced with cleats and supports, will safely hold large potted plants. Made of cedar, the plant stand looks great in doors, but it can also be placed on a patio or deck, where it will age naturally to a weathered gray. To enhance its rustic beauty, we created decorative diamond cutouts by gang-cutting notches in the side pieces, then rounded the shelf corners with a belt sander.

OVERALL SIZE:
25⅞" HIGH
14⅝" WIDE
36" DEEP

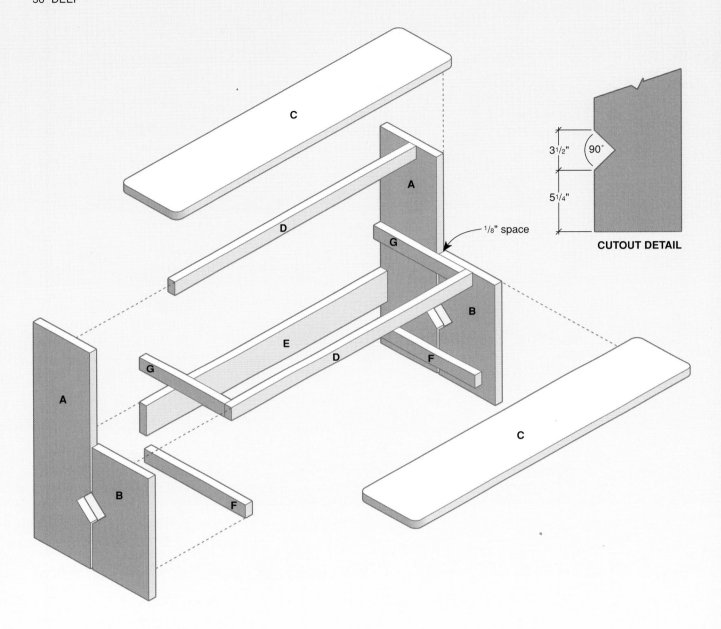

CUTOUT DETAIL

3½"

90°

5¼"

⅛" space

Cutting List				
Key	**Part**	**Dimension**	**Pcs.**	**Material**
A	Long side	⅞ × 7¼ × 25"	2	Cedar
B	Short side	⅞ × 7¼ × 14"	2	Cedar
C	Shelf	⅞ × 7¼ × 36"	2	Cedar
D	Support	⅞ × 1½ × 31¼"	2	Cedar

Cutting List				
Key	**Part**	**Dimension**	**Pcs.**	**Material**
E	Stretcher	⅞ × 3½ × 31¼"	1	Cedar
F	Long cleat	⅞ × 1½ × 13"	2	Cedar
G	Short cleat	⅞ × 1½ × 11"	2	Cedar

Materials: Waterproof wood glue, yellow deck screws (2", 1½"), finishing materials.

Note: Measurements reflect the actual thickness of dimensional lumber.

A

Mark ¾"-radius curves on the corners of the shelves, and grind them down to the lines using a belt sander.

B

Use a jig saw to gang-cut triangular notches in the side pieces, ensuring symmetrical cutouts.

Directions:
Plant Stand

MAKE THE SHELVES. Both of the shelves have rounded corners to soften the look of the project.

Start by cutting the shelves (C) to length from 1 × 8 cedar. To make the rounded corners, use a compass to draw ¾"-radius curves on the corners of both shelves. Clamp a belt sander perpendicular to your worksurface and round the corners by sanding to the lines **(photo A).**

MAKE THE SIDES. Each side has a triangle cutout that forms a diamond when the long and short sides are joined. To ensure that the diamond is symmetrical, position the long and short sides together and gang-cut the notches.

Cut the long sides (A) and short sides (B) to length. Stack a long and short side together with the edges and bottoms flush, and secure them with box tape. Mark a triangular notch on one edge (see *Diagram*); the corner of a framing square works well for marking this 90° notch.

Clamp the pieces to your worksurface and cut the notch with a jig saw. Cut matching notches on the other two side pieces, using the same procedure **(photo B).** Sand the cut edges smooth.

ATTACH THE CLEATS. Because the plant stand will inevitably come into contact with water, we used waterproof glue throughout the assembly.

Cut the long cleats (F) and the short cleats (G) to length. Lay out a long side and a short side so the edges are flush and the diamond cutout is aligned. Place ⅛" spacers between the sides. Position a short cleat

TIP

Most cedar is rough on one side. When assembling, be sure that exposed surfaces are consistent in texture. For this project, we chose to have the smooth sides facing outward.

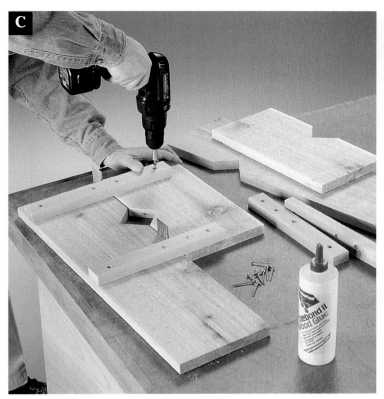

Place spacers between the sides and attach the cleats to the sides with wood glue and deck screws.

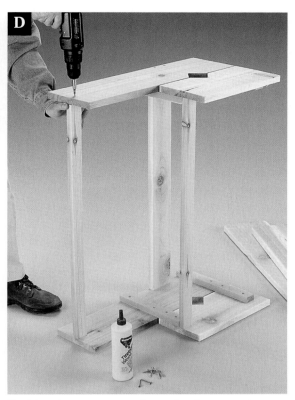

Position the supports and stretcher between the sides and join with glue and deck screws.

flush with the top edge of the short side and the back edge of the long side. Drill countersunk pilot holes through the short cleat into the sides. Attach the cleat with waterproof glue and 1½" yellow deck screws. Position a long cleat 1½" up from the bottom edges of the sides with the back edges flush. Drill countersunk pilot holes through the cleats into the sides and attach with waterproof glue and 1½" screws **(photo C)**. Remove the spacers and repeat the process for the other sides.

ATTACH THE SUPPORTS AND STRETCHER. Like the cleats, the supports and stretcher provide stability and ensure that the shelves will not bend under the weight of heavy plants.

Cut the supports (D) and stretcher (E) to length. Position the stretcher between the sides so the bottom edge is 5¼" from the bottom and the back edges are flush. Drill countersunk pilot holes through the sides into the stretcher. Attach with waterproof glue and 2" deck screws. Position the lower support against the ends of the short cleats. Drill countersunk pilot holes and attach with waterproof glue and 2" deck screws. Position the top support between the long sides and connect with waterproof glue and 2" deck screws driven through countersunk pilot holes **(photo D)**.

ATTACH THE SHELVES. Center the top shelf from side to side and drill countersunk pilot holes to connect the shelf to the side pieces. Apply glue and drive 2" deck screws through the holes. Repeat this process to attach the bottom shelf.

APPLY FINISHING TOUCHES. Scrape off any excess glue. Sand with medium-grit sandpaper to break the edges and smooth any rough spots.

> TIP
>
> *Cedar will naturally gray as it dries and weathers. If you want your cedar project to retain its original color, apply a clear wood sealer.*

Gateleg Table

Swing-out tabletop supports transform this wall-hugging oak bistro table into a full-size dining table.

CONSTRUCTION MATERIALS

Quantity	Lumber
6	1 × 4" × 8' oak
3	1 × 2" × 6' oak
1	¾" × 4 × 8' oak plywood

The gateleg table has become a standard furnishing in homes where space is tight. Typically, a gateleg table can be used as either a modest side table or, when fully extended, as a dinette-style table that seats four. This design thinks a little bigger. With the end leaves down, the tabletop measures 19 × 48" to provide plenty of space for two diners or for use as a bistro-style serving table. But when the end leaves are raised, this table expands to a spacious 67 × 48", giving you enough space for six diners with full table settings. And all this versatility is offered in a lovely oak package with fashionable slat-styling in the base.

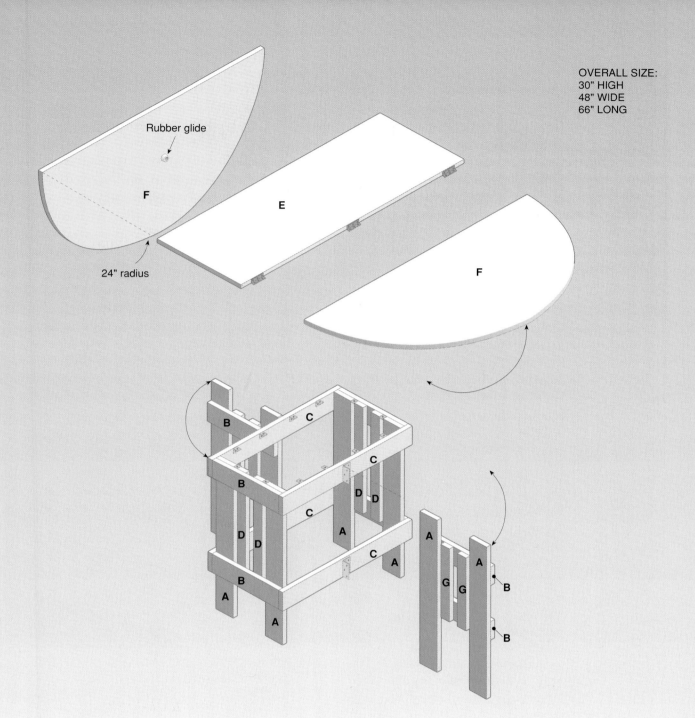

OVERALL SIZE:
30" HIGH
48" WIDE
66" LONG

Rubber glide

F

24" radius

E

F

B

C

C

D D

C

A

A

C

A

D

D

B

A

A

B

A

G G

A

B

A

B

Cutting List

Key	Part	Dimension	Pcs.	Material
A	Leg	¾ × 3½ × 29¼"	8	Oak
B	Cross rail	¾ × 3½ × 14½"	8	Oak
C	Base rail	¾ × 3½ × 28"	4	Oak
D	Base slat	¾ × 1½ × 21"	4	Oak

Cutting List

Key	Part	Dimension	Pcs.	Material
E	Table panel	¾ × 19 × 48"	1	Plywood
F	Table leaf	¾ × 24 × 48"	2	Plywood
G	Gate slat	¾ × 1½ × 14"	4	Oak

Materials: Wood glue, brass wood screws (#6 × 1¼", #6 × 2"), 1½ × 3" brass butt hinges (10), oak edge tape (25'), 1¼" brass corner braces (10), ⅞"-dia. rubber bumpers (2), finishing materials.

Note: Measurements reflect the actual size of dimensional lumber.

Attach cross rails to each pair of legs with glue and countersunk wood screws.

Position the base slats between the base legs, and attach them to the inside faces of the cross rails.

Directions:
Gateleg Table

BUILD THE LEG PAIRS. The support system for the gateleg table is made up of four pairs of 1 × 4 legs fastened to short 1 × 4 cross rails. Two of the pairs are connected with base rails to form the main table base. The swing-out gates each sport a single pair of legs. Start by cutting the legs (A) and cross rails (B) to size. Sand the parts with medium-grit sandpaper to remove any rough spots after cutting. Select four legs and four cross rails to build the leg pairs for the main base. Lay the legs flat on your worksurface, in pairs spaced about 7½" apart. Position a pair of cross rails to span across each leg pair. The ends of the cross rails should be flush with the outer edges of the legs, and the bottom of the lower cross rail should be 7¼" up from the bottoms of the legs. The upper cross rail should be flush with the tops of the legs. Use wood glue and #6 × 1¼" wood screws to attach the cross rails to each leg pair **(photo A).** Drill pilot

Sand the table base to smooth out any sharp corners or roughness.

holes for the screws, counter-bored to accept a ⅜"-dia. wood plug, and check with a square to make sure the legs and braces are at right angles to one another before you perma-nently fasten them together. Next, assemble the leg pairs for the swing-out gates the same way, except for positioning the cross rails. The bottoms of the cross rails for the gates should be 14¾" and 25¼" up from the bottoms of the legs on these pairs.

INSTALL THE SLATS. Each leg pair features two decorative slats that are attached to the in-side faces of the cross rails. Cut the 1 × 2 base slats (D) and gate slats (G) to length. Turn the base leg pairs over so the cross rails are facedown on your worksurface. Position two base slats on each leg pair so the tops of the slats are flush with the tops of the cross rails and the slats are spaced evenly, with a 1½"-wide gap between the outside edges of the slats

D

Mark the semicircular cutting line for the first table leaf with a bar compass (we made ours from a 25"-long piece of scrap wood).

TIP

Use very fine (400- to 600-grit) synthetic steel wool to buff your project between topcoats. This is especially helpful when using polyurethane, which is quite susceptible to air bubbles, even when very light coats are applied. Be sure to wipe the surface clean before applying the next coat.

and the inside edges of the legs. Use pieces of scrap 1 × 2 as spacers. Attach the slats to the cross rails with glue and #6 × 1¼" wood screws driven through counterbored pilot holes **(photo B).** Set the gate slats on the gates with the same spacing between slats, and the tops and bottoms of the slats flush with the tops and bottoms of the cross rails. Attach the gate slats to the gate cross rails with glue and screws.

ASSEMBLE THE TABLE BASE. The table base consists of the two pairs of base legs, connected by 1 × 4 side rails. Cut the base rails (C) to length, then drill a pair of counterbored pilot holes ⅜" in from both ends of each base rail. Prop the leg pairs in an upright position on a flat surface. Apply wood glue to the ends of the base cross rails, then clamp the side rails in position so the ends are flush with outer faces of the cross rails and the tops are aligned. Make sure all the joints are square, then drive #6 × 2" wood screws at each joint. After the glue in the joints has dried, apply glue to ⅜"-dia.

wood plugs and insert them into the counterbored screw holes. When the glue has dried, sand the plugs down so they are level with the surrounding wood. If the plugs are protruding more than ⅟₁₆" above the wood, use a belt sander with an 80- to 120-grit sanding belt to level off the plug, but be careful not to scuff up the faces of the rails **(photo C).**

MAKE THE TABLETOP. The tabletop top is made from three

pieces of plywood, trimmed with edge veneer tape. The rectangular table panel is mounted on the table base, and the end leaves are rounded, then attached to the table panel with butt hinges. Start by cutting the table panel (E) and table leaves (F) to the full measurements shown in the *Cutting List* on page 157. Use a bar compass to draw a centered, 24"-radius semicircle on one long edge of each leaf. If you don't own a bar compass, create a makeshift one from a 25"-long piece of straight scrap wood. Simply drill a ⅜"-dia. hole with a centerpoint ½" in from one end of the scrap to hold a pencil, then drive a 4d finish nail through a point ½" in from the other end. Attach the

E

Use an iron to apply oak veneer edge tape to all plywood edges.

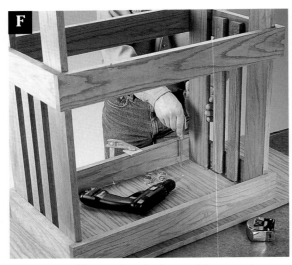

Attach the table panel to the base with corner braces.

Attach the leaves to the table panel with 1½ × 3" brass butt hinges.

finish nail to a piece of ply-wood butted against one long edge of the leaf, insert the pencil into the hole, and draw the semicircle **(photo D).** Carefully cut the semicircle with a jig saw. To even out the cut, clamp a belt sander with a 120-grit belt to your worksurface so the belt is perpendicular to the surface and can spin unobstructed. Lay the table leaf flat on the worksurface (this is very important) and gently press the rounded edge of the leaf up against the spinning belt. Move

the board back and forth across the belt until the edges are smooth and there are no irregularities in the semicircle. Use this table leaf as a template for tracing a matching semicircle onto the other leaf, then cut and shape the leaf the same way. Finally, press self-adhesive oak veneer edge tape onto all the edges of the table panel and the table leaves, using a household iron at low to medium heat setting **(photo E).** Trim off any excess tape with a sharp utility knife.

ASSEMBLE THE GATELEG TABLE. Before assembling the table parts, apply wood stain and a topcoat product (we used water-based poly-urethane) to the parts, following the manufacturer's directions. After the finish has dried, position the top panel facedown on your worksurface. Center the table base on the underside of the top panel, and attach the parts with 1¼" brass corner braces **(photo F).** Next, butt the table leaves against the sides of the top panel, and fasten each leaf with two evenly spaced 1½ × 3" brass butt hinges **(photo G).** Attach a butt hinge to the outer face of each base rail, for attaching the gates. The hinges should be aligned, and positioned so the gate will be centered exactly on the rail. Attach a gate to each table side, making sure the tops of the gate and base are flush. Open the gates and extend them so they are perpendicular to the table base. Attach a ⅞"-dia. rubber glide to the underside of each leaf as a stop to keep the gate from swinging open too far **(photo H).**

Attach rubber glides to the tabletop to work as stops for the gates.